The Battlefield of Brunanburh

The Case For Wirral

by

David P Gregg

Green Man Books

The Battlefield of Brunanburh
Published by Green Man Books 2021
15 Poulton Green Close, Spital, Wirral
CH63 9FS (davidgregg@ talktalk.net)

Copyright © David P Gregg 2021

ISBN 979 8594416499

To the men of Mercia and Wessex who fought and
fell at Brunanburh to forge the English nation as a
political entity. To the men of Ireland, Alba, Wales
and Strathclyde who fought, in part, to remind the
Anglo-Saxon & Norse newcomers that the blood of
these Islands goes back to the First Farmers and
the Megalith Builders. It still does, despite the recent
attempts to rewrite and denigrate our history and
to devalue our ancient birthrights. We must respect
those birthrights and value our heritage to deserve
the honour of being called 'British'.

Printed by Kindle Direct Publishing .
Available from Amazon Books,
The author and retail outlets

The Battle of Brunanburh on Wirral

Contents

		Page
Section 1	An Overview	4
Section 2	Preliminary Note on Recent Local Finds	27
Section 3	Defining the Battlefield Extent	35
3.1	The Northern Battle Area around Storeton	36
3.2	Escape to the West from Storeton & Brimstage	45
3.3	South of the Main Battle Area : Vingarda	57
3.4	East of the Main Battle Area	69
3.5	A Final Suggestion	77
3.6	The Dingesmere Problem	78
3.7	The Proposed Main Battlefield Area Defined	84
	A Tentative Central Battlefield Map	89
REFERENCES		90
A 1	Brunanburh and the Wirral Local Plan	92
A2	The Density Distribution of Norse – Irish Place Names on Wirral	98
A 3	Needwood Farm & Clatterbridge Standing Stones	100
A 4	Irby Standing Stones : western Battle escape route	114
A 5	Birkenhead Standing Stones : northern Battle escape route	119

Section 1   **An Overview:**

Brunanburh, Poulton 'Castle' and Brimstage 'Fort'

This book presents evidence for the location of the Battle of Brunanburh on Wirral based on geography, place and tithe field names in the several local languages and comparisons with the few historic sources on the battle including Egil's Saga, whose value has been under estimated. In the last few years Wirral Archaeology has carried out epic work in mid Wirral identifying a major weapon / metal recycling camp following some great battle. The hundreds of Saxon and Norse weapon finds have been dated to the 10th century. In the opinion of many experts now this battle can only have been Brunanburh which took place in 937 AD. The questions now are how big was the battlefield and can we identify its boundaries, a necessary condition for having the battlefield officially recognised, listed and protected. I hope this book will help define those boundaries and the various 'fighting retreat' routes along which the Norse-Irish-Scottish army remnants escaped to their long ships.

The author has long had an interest in Brunanburh and now finds himself almost next door to the post-battle weapon recovery camp of the victorious Mercian army on the southern edge of the battlefield. What raised him to action was the inclusion of many Green Belt farm fields covering a good fraction of the probable Brunanburh Battlefield, in the first draft Wirral Local Plan of 2019. An early version of this book was submitted to Wirral Council to warn them of the irreparable damage that would be done if these Green Belt parcels were released for housing development. To be absolutely clear: Brunanburh marked the formation of England as a unified nation and has **national heritage significance.** It is at least as important the Battle of Hastings. Such sites must be preserved for the nation and local authorities must legally take national heritage into account. To be fair to Wirral Council, confronted with the early field evidence of Wirral Archaeology, it commissioned an 'expert' archaeology / history report on the evidence. This was completed during 2020 but not released to the public despite several FOI requests and despite it being quoted in the new Local Plan formal evidence documents.

Despite a lack of public access to the report, access was given to an American historian, Professor Michael Livingston, in October 2020 who used the material in his new commercial book on Brunanburh (34). Some may find this strange indeed. Readers interested in the original Local Plan intentions, the heritage protection regulations and my objections to the various Local Plan stages should read Appendix 1.

There now appears to be compelling evidence that the Wirral peninsula was the site of the great Battle of Brunanburh at which the Mercian and Wessex forces of King Aethelstan and his brother Edmund, repulsed the Norse-Irish and Scottish alliance of King Anlaf of Dublin, King Constantine II of Alba, King Owain of the Strathclyde Welsh and the Lords of Mann. Norse settlers in Wales and probably Lancashire and Wirral were also involved. That defeat secured the future of a united, nominally Anglo-Saxon, kingdom in England.

The scale of the battle is made clear in the Anglo-Saxon Chronicle which tells us that by the day's end 'five kings, seven earls and countless of their hosts lay dead' upon the field. Some Irish accounts claim 35,000 dead and that the Norse allies supposedly arrived in over 600 ships. The site of the battle on Wirral is logical since the northern half of the peninsula (and likely more) was occupied by Norse-Irish settlers and the south half by the original Romano-British population and some Anglo-Saxon incomers. Ironically it was King Aethelstan's aunt, Aethelfleda, The Lady of Mercia, who gave land in north Wirral to Norse-Irish settlers from Dublin in ~902 AD. They expressed their gratitude after several years by attacking Chester but were repulsed. Aethelfleda, no doubt thinking ahead, set out to refortify a number of defensive Iron Age hill forts in Cheshire. This was both a defensive and expantionist strategy. The author wonders if she also rebuilt strong old points at Poulton Hall and Brimstage as we will see.

The Anglo-Saxons held the ancient city of Chester nearby (but with a considerable Norse trading presence). West Lancashire, Merseyside and North Wales also hosted many Norse settlements. However over forty sites have been proposed for the battle (as discussed in ref. 1).

The nub of the identification problem is that through the 10th century a number of significant conflicts occurred involving the same protagonists: the family of Anlaf of Dublin (late of Northumbria) and his Scottish allies and the family of Aethelstan of Mercia. A number of 'revolts' and serious battles took place in Northumbria and elsewhere against Mercian rule in the decades before and after Brunanburh in 937 AD (2). It may be that later commentators conflated several conflicts. For example in 934 AD the Anglo Saxon Chronicle tells of Aethelstan going north to invade Scotia with a huge army and his navy (15). He supposedly marched across Scotland to the northernmost point of Britain. By 935 AD he had subdued Constantine and 'five kings' came south (and east from Wales) to pay him homage, yet two years later, Constantine was in revolt and joined Anlaf's invasion. The final defeat of these lesser kings established England as a united kingdom and set the pattern of domination of these islands for the next millennium. Aethelstan after Brunanburh could rightly style himself as King of Britain as his coinage, minted at Chester, Winchester and other towns, famously declared.

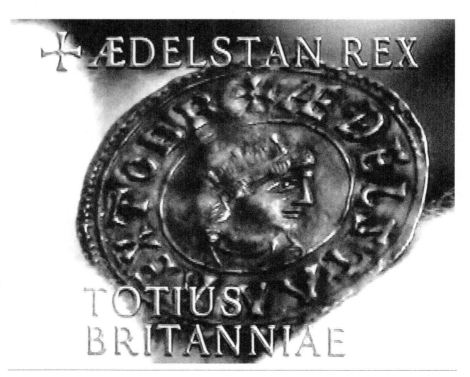

We should remember if cheering for Aethelstan that the Celtic lords of Scotland, Wales and Ireland represented the original population of these islands going back to the Iron Age and before that to the First Farmers and the Megalith Builders. The Romans spread only a thin veneer of their imperial model over very old blood. The Anglo-Saxons and the Norsemen were also new comers. The author notes this as a typical north Briton with ~70% of his DNA shared with the so-called 'Celts' of Ireland, Scotland and Wales. I take comfort that warlord invaders and their elites may come and go but the old blood endures… so far. DNA surveys confirm this.

We will not refight the location options of Brunanburh here but looking at Egil's Saga (3), attributed to the warrior scald who fought on Aethelstan's side at Brunanburh, examining many local place names and the new material discoveries, the Wirral battle site evidence is now extremely strong: see sections 2 & 3.

The Wirral Norse-Irish settlers in the 10th century had their own local parliament at Thingwall in the west. Across the River Mersey was a second settlement of Norse farmers and a second Thing a few miles inland. Talacre on the Welsh Dee coast was also Norse. Invaders sailing straight across the Irish Sea from Dublin to Wirral would find a Norse speaking and presumably supportive population. There were also several places around the Dee and Mersey suitable for landing many ships and large armies: Wallasey Pool; the 'Viking' port at Meols; Dawpool and several small ports on the Dee; Tranmere inlet and beaches; Bromborough Pool and Mersey inlets, and across the Mersey, Knott's Hole and Jericho Beach at the Dingle. There was space enough for the 615 ships of Anlaf's combined fleet which Symeon of Durham claims.

One of the unresolved issues of Brunanburh is the location of 'Dingesmere', across which Anlaf fled by ship after the great battle, according to the Anglo Saxon Chronicle. In Section 3.6 a simple solution will be offered based on the above material. This toponym and geographical analysis, in the author's opinion, firmly nails down Brunanburh's location on the Wirral and the local folklore and recent material finds confirm it.

It seems most likely as Professor Harding has claimed, that the Brunanburh 'battlefield' covered an extended area from Storeton / Higher Bebington southwards through Clatterbridge and Brakenwood and on through Poulton Lancelyn. We can imagine Anlaf's troops marching south from Meols, Wallasey Pool and the Tranmere area, and perhaps east from Dawpool and west from Bromborough Pool, to converge near Storeton, the great settlement, in Old Norse. Local tradition and field names centre the fighting below the slopes west and south of Storeton Woods (see section 3) and at Brackenwood just to the east. But whence came the Anglo-Saxons? Where were they camped? The boundary of the Norse – Irish enclave and the Saxon lands is uncertain despite the existence of Raby, the supposed boundary settlement in Old Norse, a few miles south of Brakenwood. The boundary also probably shifted over time and may have been fairly informal during peaceful periods (4 ; Ingimund was allowed to settle in the Wirral by Queen Aethelfleda around 902 AD and Anlaf invaded in 937 AD).

The density of Norse place names across Wirral tells a complex story. Almost certainly Bebington was Saxon in this period. There was a Saxon church there (although unusually, dedicated to St. Andrew) and there appears to have been an early Saxon (and Celtic?) church and convent at Bromborough but many Norse place names also existed there (see section 2). If we accept the 'simple' border story, Brimstage would also be firmly in the Norse enclave but clearly it is not simple. The only account of the battle with geographical details occurs in Egil's Saga written down formally in the early 13th century.

Egil gives information on the preparations for the battle including an apparent truce to negotiate the place and terms of conflict. Anlaf camps in a town north of the 'heath' battle site and sends men south to lay out the field with hazel rods. Aethelstan's forward men were camped to the south of Anlaf and south of the heath between a river and a large wood on raised ground. His men report to the Norsemen that the King would soon, in a few days, come from the town several hours ride to the south of the heath site. Was this perhaps Chester? Meanwhile the forces gathered.

Was Anlaf's camp on the high, easily defended, ground at Storeton village, which had clear access north to Tranmere inlet and Wallasey Pool along the Roman road, and to Thingwall and the west coast, with excellent views southwards? Several analysts have claimed that this eastern Roman road passed through Storeton and Prenton (8) and on to Wallasey Pool where the remains of a 'Roman' (but possibly medieval) bridge / jetty were discovered in the mid 19th century. Perhaps Aethelstan's main army came up the route of the same Roman Road from Chester? Some colleagues believe the king brought true cavalry for the first time, and surprised the Norsemen. We should also note that the standard levy, skeid longships of the invaders carried two horses as standard.

'Round Brunanburh' circa 1900

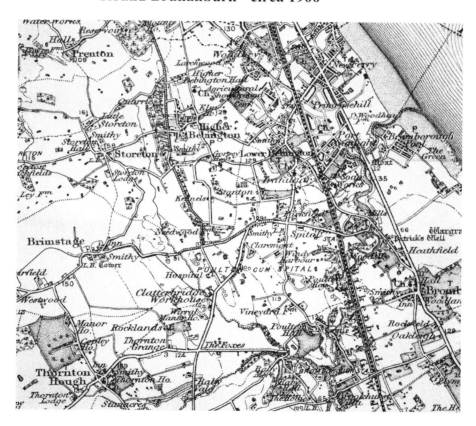

Athelstan's men awaited their king on land between a river and a large wood, south of the heath.

Well, west and south of Spittle Heath (Brackenwood) we have the Clatterbook running into the Dibbin (perhaps the Vina of Egil; see section 3). The wood is not helpful in placing the site: much of the area had woods and Storeton Hill and Poulton Lancelyn still do. But a wood on a raised site could be related to the high ground at Poulton Lancelyn and Vineyard Farm. When Aethelstan arrived it seems logical that he would encamp his main army near existing strong points. Historically attention has been focused on Bromborough because of the name itself: Brunanburh, Bruna's stronghold. Bruna is an Old English personal name. But remember also the clear cluster of Norse place names at Bromborough. By Bromborough Pool courthouse there were ancient earthworks which were long *assumed* to be that stronghold. Did *some* of Anlaf's fleet land at the Pool and reoccupy old earthworks? We will see conflict evidence here later.

A little to the north east of the current village, old OS and tithe maps marked three fields as 'wargraves' and associated them with the battle of Brunanburh. Was this a belated fight for the Pool? But the area of 'Bromborough' even in the 19th century, as marked on early OS maps, stretched far to the west of the current village. Also Anlaf was camped 'north' of the heath battle site and 'north' of Aethelstan's forward camp, not east of it, according to Egil. A mile to the south west of the Pool is higher ground at Poulton Lancelyn surrounded on three sides by the deep valley of the Clatterbrook and Dibbin.

At Poulton Hall the Lancelyn Greens have held the land since the Norman Conquest. An old family tradition says that a castle once stood there on the promontory ridge and indeed a 'castle' is marked on early OS maps. However no heavy duty masonry has ever been found there. This does not preclude a large earth and wooden stockade enclosure in Saxon times. Perhaps this was the eastern stronghold of Bruna? This place is indeed 'south' of Spittle Heath and Storeton woods. But there is another site of interest.

A mile west of the often presumed battlefield centre at Clatterbridge , a mile south southwest of Storeton and two and a half miles west of Bromborough village, lies the ancient village of Brimstage. It is well known for the medieval tower and hall which holds a grinning feline carving said to have inspired the Cheshire Cat.

There are also the remains of a modest moat. However its origins may be far older and it may be our missing 'Saxon' western stronghold. The geography is striking. The main road performs an accurate semicircle (of about 700 ft diameter) to avoid a north facing, high, steep bank of exposed sandstone which is largely natural (Figure 1).

Figure 1   Brimstage Village in 1872

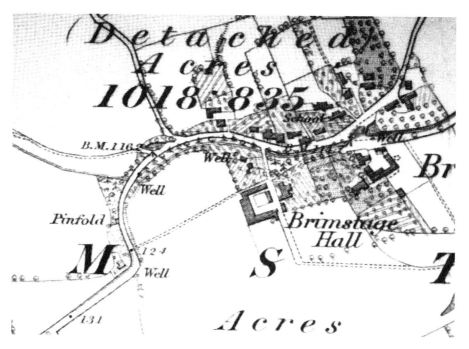

A deep stream flows along its base. The medieval tower and hall are on the eastern boundary of the circle. The author has long wondered about this landform. It is reminiscent of a low level, so called 'Marsh Fort', as opposed to the more familiar 'Hill Fort' of Iron Age date, several of which exist in northern Cheshire, and some of which were refortified by the Mercians. There is a further low level fort on the Dee coast at Burton (Burh – tun) to the west and early 'castle' earthworks at Shotwick. The Brimstage west, north and north – east boundary is defended by the 'natural' rock walls and stream. It occurred to the author that if an earth dam was built to the east of the village and the area flooded, our circle and more would be well protected from attack from the west, north and east. It was then noted that early tithe maps mark the rock platform boundary as 'Moat Road' (Figure 2).

Figure 2 Brimstage Area Early 19th Century Tithe Map

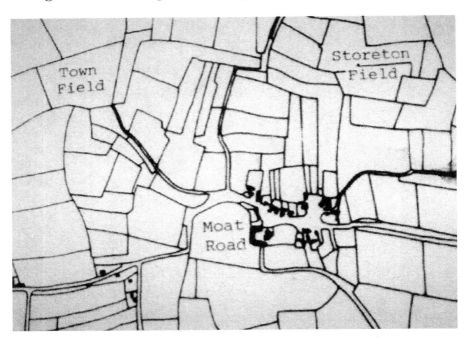

Locals know that in wet periods the 'Moat Road' still floods even without a dam. The Wirral flood risk map confirms this. The stream out of Brimstage to the east still drains a large area subject to flood risk. In fact the Clatterbrook and Dibbin streams and their feeder streams all appear on the Wirral flood risk map. Later we will argue that the Clatterbrook / Dibbin valleys marked the southern edge of the 'Plains of Othlynn' another name for the Brunanburh battlefield.

Perhaps the early settlers did create a wide protective moat at Brimstage which could double as a fishing lake. The Wirral Historic Settlement Study (December 2011) mentions a water mill north of the ancient core. Was the suggested moat also used as a mill pond at some period? Was the large moat and the outflow stream to the east, the 'river' near Athelstan's camp spoken of by Egil? (section 3).

It is interesting that the narrow Brimstage stream now runs eastwards in a very deep cutting to join the Clatterbrook and then the Dibbin. This cut (or the pre-cut marshy land) would form a distinct boundary and a considerable barrier if defended from the south side. However at Brimstage the southern half of the circular bank field was apparently unprotected.

Fortunately Lidar maps now exist for much of the Wirral including Brimstage. Figure 3 presents a blow up of this map. Several interesting landform features show up. Most notable is the broad linear earth bank which runs roughly east from the end of the rock bank boundary and disappears under current farm buildings. The bank and ditch are still prominent after several centuries of ploughing. This must once have been a formidable barrier, perhaps hosting a timber palisade. Also visible across the centre of the circular enclosure is a smaller bank and ditch which joins the road to the west to the same road east of the enclosure. A19th century footpath followed roughly the same line. At some time the road followed a straight path across the site before the fortified enclosure existed or after it was abandoned. Some colleagues in Wirral Archaeology suspect that there may have been a subsidiary Roman road here.

A 'major' Roman road (from Deva to Wallasey Pool?) is thought to pass through Clatterbridge a mile or so to the east and on or just west of the probable battle centre (8). From the centre of the enclosure a pair of parallel ditches ~17 ft apart runs to the south and across the southern boundary bank to end in the ditch. This suggests the ditches may be contemporary with the bank. We cannot be sure before excavation but here is a suggested sequence of events:

Iron Age people fortify the natural enclosure and build a farmstead. The Romans subdue the area and build a minor road across the site. After the legions leave the Romano-British re-fortify the site. Later, the incoming Saxon (and Norse?) 'invaders' also used it as a stronghold, including perhaps King Aethelstan and his army in 937 AD.

It is not however, identifiably mentioned in the sources such as Egil's Saga.

The Anglo-Saxon Chronicle speaks of the battle 'Round Brunanburh' which is also the name of the whole area. But Norse – Irish attacking from the north would find a formidable defensive position in front of them... if it was occupied at this time and coupled with the deep, eastward flowing stream.

Figure 3   Brimstage LIDAR Map

All this is but reasonable conjecture. However the local historical place names also provide support in unexpected and internally consistent ways. We noted that Bruna is an Old English name but intriguingly there are other possibilities in OE and Old Norse.

The name Brimstage appears in records from the 12th and 13th century onwards with the advent of the Domville family (5, 6). Brunstath court 1260; Brimstache 1275; Brunstach 1326; Brunstathe 1348. Other noted variants: **Brunaburgh** (cf Brunanburh); Brunanstaepa; Brunastaed (or stadr, ON for farmstead).

Several analysts have pointed out that early maps show a variety of names for our area of interest but a few 16th and 17th century maps certainly show 'Brunburgh' as its name (19).

Clearly we consistently have the apparent OE name Bruna at Brimstage. Brunstath could simply mean Bruna's place, Bruna's holding. Brunstach would be Bruna's stack, post or pillar in OE. This could imply a standing marker stone of some kind. Curiously at the north end of the village, surmounted by the little school house, is a second high sandstone platform, natural in origin but clearly reshaped. A battered standing stone is set into the bedrock there. With a dammed moat full of water this platform would edge that moat. It is a curious thing but 'brunnr' in ON is a stream. We could read the place name as the boundary stone by the stream: Brunnrstach or as Brunnrstath, the stream settlement. Also Brunaburgh could be read as Bruna's river bank in OE and Brunanstaepa as Bruna's river landing place. We should note also ON bryggja, a pier and ON bru, a causeway across marshy ground. In the latter case we could read bru-nand-burh since nand means in proximity to, near in ON, giving the Causeway Fort. It has to be said that these 'river' names could also be applied to the Poulton Hall site and the earthworks at Bromborough Pool.

The repeated theme of water is interesting. Early OS maps show several wells and springs in and around the village. Ironically the famous TV historian Michael Wood used the 'brunn', double n form to interpret the battlefield name as 'the fort at the spring'. He then announced to the media that the battle site was near Robin Hood's Well on the A1 at the village of Burghwallis (an old Roman fort site) near Doncaster (2). Nearby Barnsdale Bar Hill *would* make a good burh site and one of the other 10th century battles could have occurred here. Wood is a long term advocate of a Yorkshire location for the great battle. He dismisses the Bromborough evidence as being 'merely' based on 'the name' although his own name interpretation applies equally well or better to Brimstage where there are several springs in the village. Wood has clearly never looked at the Wirral landscape nor it seems have proponents of other sites. Even so there are many streams and springs on Wirral and many settlement sites. The name, if given to a whole area, would surely need to have had something more distinctive and unique about it?

Well 'brun' in ON can also be a cliff or edge so that heidar – brun is the edge of a heath (see also Appendix 1). But a distinctive, natural, semi-circular cliff edge is *exactly* what we have at Brimstage (11). Brunstath would be the place (or farmstead) on the cliff. Brunstache would be the pillar cliff, or better, a cliff stack since a stack is a rock pillar (surrounded by water). The Wirral we must remember was Celtic before the Saxons and Norse came. We should not neglect the Celtic languages. In Irish one interpretation of 'bru' (from OI bruig) means brink, verge, bank of a river. Interestingly the plural form is brunna. However in Irish bru (plural bruna) is also a hall or hostel as in Bru na Boinne, the Mansions of the Boyne, the great semi-circular Bend of the Boyne which encloses ancient Newgrange. So we could read Brun na burh as the fort on the brink, on the cliff edges, on the river (moat) bank. In English we still have brow as in the brow or edge of a hill. Synonyms include verge, brink and brim... The edge, brink, cliff, interpretation of Brunanburh can be applied to Brimstage and to the Poulton Hall site but not perhaps to Bromborough Pool.

The problem with interpreting names in any language is the breadth of meanings which can become attached to a word or very similar words. We have seen several meanings attached to brun. Here is one more: a brun is an eyebrow.

If we look at the lidar image of old Brimstage it is indeed eyebrow shaped! Was brun a local nick name? But above we already noted, bru and brow meaning edge, brink. Here is another coincidence: we noted burh and burgh names in this context but there is also bughr in ON which remarkably, means curve. So Brunbughr is an eyebrow curve. Perhaps though, we should stick to the several water related and cliff / edge words at this point.

If the cliff enclosure at Brimstage was indeed fortified (and perhaps several times over the centuries) it would be doubly distinctive and could, in Saxon/Norse times, have become known as Brun(an)burh: the fort on the cliff edge or Cliff Fort. What about the 'an' element? If Bruna was a personal name brunan would be the genitive singular form in OE : Bruna's Fort. However it is claimed that 'an' in OE also signifies big or notable...famous. We could have a conflation of Brunburh and Brunanburh over time. Brunanburh is certainly as easy to say.

The known existence of several name variants with elements with several (often related) meanings in local languages would certainly promote this kind of conflation. Some early forms also include Brynstath and so on. Bryn is OW, a hill or mount, which could apply to our raised stone cliff. However we also note ON brynja which means armour, chain mail, protection. So we have an armoured or protected place...or, as we might say, a fort or burh.

Such a strong fort would naturally dominate the area, including the nearest natural river port at modern Bromborough Pool, and *also* bestow its name widely on the local land. Some earthwork defences at the Pool might be expected. Similarly, the Poulton Hall site could have provided an eastern, defended outpost. In the early decades of the 10th century we also know that Aethelfleda, Lady of the Mercians, formidable aunt of Aethelstan, refortified some hill forts in west Cheshire in response to the Norse threat. She allowed Ingimund and his followers to settle in north Wirral in 902 AD but he grew greedy for more land. After he attacked Chester did she also refortify Brimstage and the Poulton Hall site? She refortified Chester itself in 907 and Eddisbury hill fort in west Cheshire in 914 and Runcorn fort in 915 AD (14; but see section 3also).

The place name analysis of section 3 shows how we can relate Poulton Lancelyn to place names which occur in the historical sources and sagas. Many of these names are conflict related. Vineyard Farm is compatible with the 'Vinheidi' battle site name of Egil's Saga : 'Vina River Heath'. Vineyard becomes Vina gardr', the 'Vina River Enclosure (Fort)'. The Poulton Hall site and the adjacent farm are enclosed by the deep valleyed, Clatterbrook and Dibbin . That would make these streams equal to the Vina of Egil. But Vina could also be the name of the feeder streams of the northern Clatterbrook and Brimstage. As we will show in section 3 this is an excellent name to attach to streams flowing through a battle field. We note OE clatra and ON klattra, meaning 'a noisy commotion', a loud noise 'as of hard objects striking rapidly against each other'. We also note ON, klaka, a dispute. Much more new name evidence for the area is presented in section 3, involving conflict related terms in ON, OI and OE (including Bowman, Pikes and Welsh Graves, Greets (lament), Iver (archer), Areid (cavalry charge), Leita a (attack), Hogg (blow, execution, behead), Lamper (beat, lame), Galla (scream), Faugh (OI battle cry), Egg (edge, sword) and so on.

We also note less certainly, the place of the battle named in later Irish sources on the 'Plaines of Othlyn' (Annals of Clonmacnoise). 'Oth' has been read as 'od' meaning 'up to'. Linn in Gaelic and llyn in Welsh mean a pool, lake, stream or a 'deep place' in a river. So we have a plain 'up to' the boundary of a river for the battle field name. We noted earlier that 'heidar brun' meant the edge of a heath and Egil gave us Vinheidr for the battle name: the Vina river heath. Putting both names together gives us Vinheidarbrun: Vina heath boundary. This seems curiously close to the standard interpretation of the Plaines of Othlyn. In section 3 we discuss the word odr which means raging, berserk, which could give us the 'Plains of the River of Rage' (the Clatterbrook?). This all seems to relate readily to Egil's description of rivers and heaths. Now Poulton Lancelyn still has several meres and streams in deep cuttings. Half a mile south west of Poulton Hall we have the larger Raby Mere, a third of a mile long. This is the largest mere by far on Wirral. In early sources the area appears as Poltune: the settlement by the pool or lake.

In conclusion I suggest the main battle and camps area lay south of the Storeton / Higher Bebington line and east of Brimstage and the deep stream bed running from Brimstage to Clatterbridge. The southern boundary then followed the deep Clatterbrook / Dibbin Valley across to Poulton Hall on its high promontory in the east. This would put the geographical battle activity centre somewhere near Brakenwood, and the area west at Clatterbridge, as Professor Harding has claimed. However we will see evidence for significant conflicts along obvious escape routes for the defeated Norse – Irish to the north, west and probably east.

Egil's Saga may provide one last tentative indicator as to location. He tells of the flight of Earl Aelfgir from the first preliminary clash at Brunanburh between Anlaf's forces, under the turncoat earls, Adil & Hring, opposing the forces of Aelfgir (and Egil) before the arrival of King Aethelstan. Hard pressed, Aelfgir losses his nerve and flees. 'He rode to the southlands and of his travels tis to be told he rode night and day til he came westward to the Earl's Ness.'
This was a fateful decision because Egil's forces rally and defeat Adil and Hring's men and begin a great slaughter of the Norse, pursuing them northwards through the woods. Aelfgir, fleeing south, comes near to the town where Aethelstan is waiting (Chester?) but fears to meet the King and turns west to the 'Earl's Ness'. This would put the battle site north east of the 'Earl's Ness'. From the port at the Ness Aelfgir takes a ship to France from where he never returns to Britain.

If we consult an OS map of Wirral and trace lines south westwards and south south westwards from Brakenwood / Poulton to the west coast we hit the villages of Neston, Little Neston and Ness. On the coast between Little Neston and Ness stands Denhall Quay. Denhall according to Harding, is ON Danir meaning Dane and hall is suggested to be ON waella, spring, by Harding. However, hallr, is a hill or big stone or flat rock in ON. This could well describe the rocky headland at Denhall. Ness itself of course is a nose or headland in ON. Denhall is said to be the only Danish settlement among the many Norse settlements on the Wirral. The east side of the Dee has hosted several small ports since Roman times including Parkgate, Denhall, Burton, & Shotwick (on the old salt trail to Wales) further south.

A deep channel once ran as far as Shotwick. Denhall Quay is most probably the Earl's Ness. However, does the rest of the tale fit this area? Some have said the Earl's 'southlands' flight refers to southern England but why? Why fly southwards into the Mercian heartland? Why risk the King's wrath at Chester? Why could the southlands not just mean the lands to the south? Ness is on the usually presumed boundary of the Norse enclave. But also, Denhall is only five or so miles from Brakenwood / Poulton, a few hours ride under normal conditions. Maybe Aelfgir approached Chester before, hearing of the King's approaching main army, changes his mind and turns west, adding several miles. But conditions were not normal. Aelfgir would not wish to encounter and be recognised by Mercian patrols.

Also the battle is held to have taken place near the year's end, in mid October perhaps. If so the 'day long' battle would have ended near dusk and Aelfgir might have rode on, gratefully, through the evening avoiding the Mercian army. Egil's Saga says specifically that Aethelstan and the main army arrive at Brunanburh at night fall, as does Anlaf, from his northern camp. The main battle occurs the next morning and again the Mercians and their allies are triumphant. Anlaf flees back to Dublin across Dingesmere and King Constantine to Scotland and King Owain to Cumbria.

One of the problems with the identification of the battle site on Wirral is John of Worcester's mention of Anlaf's forces coming by ship to the Humber. There were several significant battles in the 10th century to confuse later chroniclers. However this issue may have already been resolved over a century ago by Francis Tudsbury of Oriel College, Oxford (9). In the presumed main day of battle, Aethelstan makes his own stand in fields between the foot of Humbersdon, a high hill, and a river. Well, just northwest of the old Needwood Farm site at Brackenwood is Umberstone Covert, a wood covering the old Roman quarry site on a hill slope. The name similarity is obvious. But there was indeed once a large stone at the mouth of the Humber: the Humberstone. However the name and several variants of it occurred very early in other places, Herefordshire and Leicestershire for example. Humber or Umber is a fairly common river name. It probably derives from the Latin, Umbra: shadow, darkness.

Also, adjacent Brackenwood is, perhaps, the wood on the slope from ON brekka, a slope or hill. But note also brokon, brokun, clashing in ON: The Clashing Wood? Just west of mount Road is the Pingle. This can mean a small field. However note also ON pina, to mortify and in Gaelic archaic dialect, a fierce struggle or quarrel. To the west is the similarly named Clatterbrook we tentatively identified as part of the Vina river. The ground by the stream was probably marshy. It is still remembered perhaps, at Sitch Cottages at junction 4 of the M53. A tithe field just to the west was also called Sitch. Sitch is from Sike in OE meaning slow flowing water. Sich is also an old surname attached to a person living by a marshy stream or damp gully. The area nearby is rich in Old Norse names. We also have Sour Flat but ON saur means mud, filth; good names for marshy ground. However we also have saera and soera meaning wound and sarr meaning wounded. We also have the intriguing Leather Sitch. We note ON leita a, to attack, to assault. Also leidr, meaning hateful and letja, meaning hinder, obstruct and leifa, meaning to abandon, to leave, *after death*. There are other suggestive area names considered in section 3.

This area just west and east of M53 junction 4 may be a centre of battle action. The battle is also said to have occurred 'where two streams meet'. We have the Clatterbrook flowing south here meeting the deep stream from Brimstage flowing south eastwards. The streams met where Clatterbridge Hospital now stands. Just to the north another stream, still subject to occasional flooding, joins the Clatterbrook. Near this, close to the hospital we also have Round Hey, no. 252. Curiously this is not round but very irregular in shape. Please note that in ON a rond is a shield. By the old Clatterbridge workhouse site (known as 'The Spike') we have plot no. 182, Nog Meadow. In OE and Nose dialect hnoc is a hook or bent implement but see below. In OI we have 'Tir na Nog' the paradise of eternal youth guarded by the Fianna, protectors of Ireland. Also note ON nagrindr, gates of the dead. Just to the west, along Brimstage Road, we have plots 138, Hooks and 140, Hookes. In ON we have hogg, blow, behead, execution; hoggva to slaughter; hogg orrosta, meaning close hand to hand fighting. But we also have haukr in ON, hauk in ME from hafoc in Old Saxon meaning hawk, but also 'a young and brave man'; 'warlike'.

In ME a hauk is a hook shaped tool used in thatching and a later tool used in plastering. Note OD hnukko and Icelandic hnokki meaning hook. Synomyms collected from various dictionaries include: hack, cutter, knife, bodkin and cleaver. We may reasonably infer a weapon connection with this site.

A little further west we have a number of Dob Meadows (27, 135, 142). In OE, Swedish and Icelandic we have dubba, dub, to strike (with a sword). By Storeton village we also have field 122, Doubloons with possibly the same meaning: Dob loons (selions).

What about the area west of the northern Clatterbook, east of Brimstage and south of Storeton? There is more level, dry ground here for a fight and it includes the proposed Roman road line. Did Athelstan's mounted troops also follow that line northwards? We speculated earlier that Anlaf had followed the same road line south from Wallasey Pool. He may have brought many horses on his levy longships (see below). The area would be better ground for cavalry than the (presumed) marshy land adjacent to the northern Clatterbrook and the stream flowing south eastwards from Brimstage to Clatterbridge. Near Hooks where Brimstage Road turns suddenly north and then westwards, we have three fields called White Leys (nos. 173, 174, 184) running south to north on the possible Roman road line. We noted above, ON vaeta meaning stain (as in vaettfang, battle) but also vaettr, spirit. But vaeta verbally, is pronounced white. Did we have vaettr leys, spirit fields or the stained (with blood) fields? But in ON lae, pronounced lie perhaps, means harm, destruction, misfortune. Did we have vaett laes, stains of destruction, or spirits of misfortune? We seem to have coherent clusters of conflict names. However I also note the name Iveston Farm just north of Brimstage village, date unknown. Do we have Ive(r)s tun? Tun is a farm. Iver, Ivarr, Ivor etc, are derived from yr – herr, in ON, meaning yew (bow) warrior, or archer: the farm of the archers? Note that herr also means a host, an army.

It is worth noting that in some sources one of the 'kings' who died in the battle was Ivarr, son of the Danish King. From the 1839 tithe map we may also note the field (no. 125) called simply 'Pikes'. South of Brimstage, south west of the hospital, there are field nos. 228, 230, Pike Hey.

OE pic is point, prick. The pike (fish) was named for its pointed jaw. In ON a pic is a pointed peak. There are no peaks nearby, leaving the weapon name. Both sides certainly had long thrusting spears. The chief Norse god, Odin, was 'Lord of the Spear'. Did some of the Saxon host, or the Norse, camp here, near Bruna's Fort before the battle? Just west of Brimstage we also note Whitehouse Lane of unknown date. In ON vitr is white but viti means misfortune, punishment. Vaett is also pronounced white & vaettfang is a battle. In ON hauss means a skull (see section 3 for more discussion of Norse escape routes to the west).

In the Anglo-Saxon Chronicle, the epic poem, 'The Battle of Brunanburh', locates the battle as 'Round Brunanburh' suggesting an extended area of conflict as Harding has long maintained (4, 7). We also noted that Brimstage was long part of Bromborough parish. However it is curious that the sources do not *stress* any obvious strong points including our proposed 'burhs' at Brimstage and Poulton. Were these sites unoccupied and derelict at this time? Had the area been quiet for some decades after Aethelfleda had repulsed Wirral's Ingimund attacks and refortified Chester in 907 AD? Certainly there was a considerable settled Norse, 'business' population at Chester by the time of Brunanburh according to Harding (19). Or did the two *fully manned* burhs merely provide a minor backdrop to the drama given the immense scale of the battle? This could be so if Anlaf and his allies really came with 615 warships, according to Symeon of Durham. Is Symeon describing our battle? Is this number credible? Well, we have the forces of three major warlord kings to consider along with lesser followers. Around 1050 King Sven Estridsson of Denmark had 720 ships at his command. In the 12th century the levy fleet was nominally 900 ships strong (10). The invasion fleet of Harald Hardrada in 1066 is also revealing. The Anglo Saxon Chronicle describes the fleet as

'a very great sea force, with 300 ships or more.'

Heimskringla Saga says the fleet involved well over 200 ships besides 'provision ships and small craft.'(21). In the case of Anlaf's invasion we have the combined forces of three kingdoms: Dublin, Alba (Scotland) and Strathclyde and the lesser Lords of Mann and so on.

Three fleets of 200 ships gives us 600; not far from the 615 given by Symeon.

Anlaf and Constantine knew the English had a powerful fleet. The safe move was to bring many warships and supply ships. The biggest warships were called *drekar*, dragons. The biggest Norwegian ships carried a crew of ~100 men. The typical levy longship was a *skeid*, which means sword shaped. Such ships carried forty four men and two horses. The big ships typically carried thirty pairs of oars, sixty men at least (10). 615 skeids would hold 27,000 men and 1,230 horses. 615 *drekar* would hold 36,900 men. Being conservative, 400 *skeids* would imply 17,600 men. This does not include the men of local chiefs in Wirral, south Lancashire and north Wales who chose to join Anlaf. It is said that Aethelstan also came with a mighty host of men. Since he won the day let us assume a number at least the equal of Anlaf's army, say 20,000. However, William of Malmesbury, in 1127, claimed Aethelstan could gather a national levy army of 100,000 men! Maybe, but not at short notice. Perhaps then the various chroniclers did not greatly exaggerate with ~40,000 men in total in conflict 'Round Brunanburh' (see the note on recent weapons finds below). It is interesting given these outline calculations to look at what the various sources record while noting that some were written centuries later. Begin with the Anglo Saxon Chronicle which says

'Five young kings lay dead upon the battlefield, by swords
Sent to their final sleep; and likewise seven
Of Anlaf's earls, and countless of his host,
Both Scots and seamen.'

'...Nor has there on this island
Been ever yet a greater number slain,
Killed by the edges of the sword before
This time, as books make known to us...'

In the late 900s the royal chronicler Aethelweard recorded that the common people (presumably of the region concerned) still called Brunanburh 'The Great Battle' which, given the several major battles of the 10th and 11th centuries between Saxons and Norsemen, might be taken as mass expert testimony!

Henry of Huntingdon records this dark piece:

'Then the dark raven with horned beak,
And the livid toad, the eagle and kite,
The hound and wolf in mottled hue,
Were long refreshed by these delicacies.
In this land no greater war was ever waged.'

The Annals of Ulster tell us

'A huge war, lamentable and horrible, was cruelly waged between
Saxons and Norsemen. Many thousands of Norsemen, beyond
number died although King Anlaf escaped with a few men. While a
great number of the Saxons also fell on the other side, Aethelstan
king of the Saxons, was enriched by the victory.'

Is it possible that there *were* 34,800 Scots and Norse (and Saxon?)
casualties as the Annals of Clonmacnoise insist? The recent weapon
recovery site described below and the number of weapons found
does support the idea of tens of thousands of fighters. It may also be
significant that Anlaf brought over his invasion forces in October.
The harvest was just a month before. He could bring large food
supplies with him *and* know that the friendly Norse farmers of
Wirral and Lancashire would have large food stocks in preparation
for winter. A large invasion army could have beeen supported.
937 AD was during the Medieval Climate Maximum so October
weather then would be milder than now on average and harvests
good. It was the MCM which generally supercharged the
Scandinavian expansion across Europe and into the Americas.

After the Brunanburh Battle, unified England (except, periodically,
'Anlaf's' rebellious Northumbria) became more peaceful and forts
perhaps, less important. England existed for a time under the rule
King Canute but it was always England. An early pre-conquest
Saxon (Celtic?) church and convent supposedly existed at the
village now called Bromborough, close to the River Mersey and to
Bromborough Pool. In 912 Aethelfleda, The Lady of Mercia
(daughter of Alfred the Great, aunt and guardian of Aethelstan)
is also said to have founded a small monastic settlement at
Bromborough but this is disputed.

The Saxon church was ceded to St Werburgh's Abbey in 1152. Part remained visible until 1828. The chronicler Aethelweard (Aethelstan's nephew?), who reported in 980 AD that Brunanburh was still called the 'Great Battle' a generation later by the common people, and also says patriotically that afterwards

'all the fields of Britain were joined into one and there was peace everywhere and an abundance of all things.'

During the Medieval Climate Maximum we should expect good harvests as note earlier. 'Abundance' might be accurate reporting. Edward I (Longshanks) gave a charter granting a three day fair in June to the monks at Bromborough village in 1278. It became an important market 'town' then. Peace, religion and trade moved the focus away from the fortified Brunanburh at Brimstage (or Poulton Lancelyn, or both) to the present Bromborough village site. Were the early, possibly key roles of the 'Cliff Fort' and 'Poulton Castle' largely forgotten, except in local traditions and tithe field names? Perhaps. After the Norman Conquest the incoming noble families presumably felt the need for some security. At Brimstage the high, impressive, defensive tower and moat were built in the 13th century and in the 14th, the stout, stone built hall, but the massive old cliff enclosure was never refortified by the Domvilles or later landowners. The Battle of Brunanburh was forgotten, except in local legends, river, wood and field names, in sporadic weapon finds and scattered bones and despite its important role in the consolidation of the English Nation.

Section 3 looks in much more detail at the place name and tithe field name evidence for the main battle area but also explores the possible Norse escape routes from the main battle site to Meols, Dawpool, Wallasey Pool, Tranmere Inlet and Bromborough Pool. These are the places where the Norse - Irish – Scottish fleets may have landed their armies and where the defeated forces of Anlaf sought out the ships for home and safety as the Anglo Saxon Chronicle tells us. All would be well known to the Norse locals and to regular Norse-Irish traders. The port at Meols in particular was exposed to bad weather in the Irish Sea yet the Romans, Norse and medieval traders used it for millennia. These were professional sailors and Anlaf would not have lacked for local knowledge, guides and support.

Section 2   A Preliminary Note on Recent Local Finds

In 2018 Wirral Archaeology began a systematic survey of the area around Poulton Lancelyn using metal detectors and with landowner permission. That extensive work has confirmed the presence of a major site in the area yielding a very considerable quantity of metallic artefacts such as arrow heads, bodkins, spearheads, sword fragments of the 'right' age, gaming pieces and iron billets. In all over 3,000 items were found across two fields including ~350 identifiable weapons (by late 2020) and evidence of significant metal working. The shape of the spear heads and distinctive Viking sword pommels, according to the several recognised academic experts consulted so far, indicate a major battle site with Saxon / Viking protagonists (8). In autumn 2019 Wirral Archaeology began a campaign to publicise their finds. Accounts were given to local and national newspapers and an excellent public lecture on the battle and a display of finds was given at St. Andrews Saxon church in Bebington. This was appropriate since in 1871 a mass grave of many bodies with 'battle wounds' and 'arrowheads' was found beneath the church. The author heard of these remains from the local vicar as he prepared for his marriage there in 1971. The bones are still there and may be the remains of the more important Saxon dead from the battle nearby. Wirral Archaeology has released images of the weapon finds at Poulton and these are now available on the internet and in Professor Livingston's book, via WMBC. The WMBC 'expert report is still not available to Wirral residents. A few images are presented here. The first includes arrow heads, javelin and lance heads and Viking style sword pommels. The second shows a zoomorphic strap end discovered on the site.

The author attended the Wirral Archaeology meeting with a visiting group of academic 'Viking' experts who recently examined the finds and site and gave strong verbal support. The author was given several minutes to describe his views on the area of the battlefield and on the major threat posed by the Wirral Council intention to releaseseveral large 'green belt parcels' across the battlefield
 in the new Local Plan, including the field which contains the Mercian Camp / weapon recovery site described here. WA reported that :

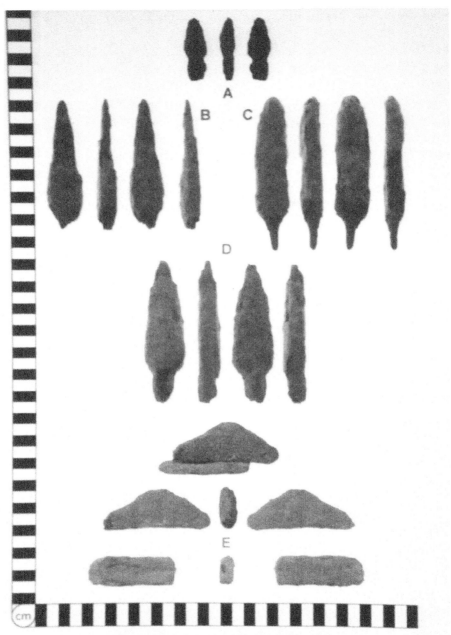

Brunanburh Battlefield Finds

'Several eminent historians and academics have examined a range of evidence we have collected, including physical artifacts and they have concluded that the lost site of the Battle of Brunanburh may have been identified by WA. There is still a great deal of investigative work that needs time to be done, and we are grateful to the group of professional archaeologists and medieval historians who are now actively assisting us.'

On a personal note : the author himself has found tantalising metal and ceramic fragments over the years, on the next field to the recovery / camp site including a forged iron mattock head of uncertain date. Such mattocks, hafted digging tools, also served as peasant military weapons in many eras from the Iron Age onwards to medieval times. However the form is similar to that used in Anglo-Saxon / Viking tools, see below. Material turns up regularly on the nearby fields. A neighbour recently made an interesting find digging in his garden on the original farm land level. It appears to be a soft stone warp weight with a carefully bored hole from a small Viking hand loom, although no doubt Saxon looms were similar at that time.

This newly discovered site is consistent with a collection point and processing camp for metal items recovered after the battle. This was an organised process at the time. The Norse similarly had the 'bera til stangar' which meant 'carry to the standard (pole)'. The enemy slain were stripped of everything useful and (in principle) 'all' was brought to the Chief's or King's standard where the spoils were assessed and distributed according to strict rules (10). The Mercians no doubt had a similar process. If this was a major recovery camp how efficient was it? Iron was valuable, hence the small smelting furnaces found on the site.

Yet ~350 weapon items from arrow heads to large spear blades were left in the ground, densely clustered in the recovery area, and over 3,000 pieces of metal in all. What percentage of the material collected from the battle site does this lost material represent? Could it be more than 3%? If not we would have 11,700 weapon items initially collected from the (local?) area of the battlefield. If each of the ~3,000 small pieces of iron was once an arrow head we would have 100,000 arrow heads. If each archer carried 24 arrows initially this yields 4,170 archers.

One assumes in addition that the individual victors also individually 'recovered' small useful items from the field such as arrows, knives, swords and javelins shortly after the battle. This was the practice. Likewise the locals, after dark, may have been out for a little (or a lot of) looting. So the material *recovered* for processing at the camp was only a fraction of that initially laying on the battlefield.

Poulton Lancelyn Mattock

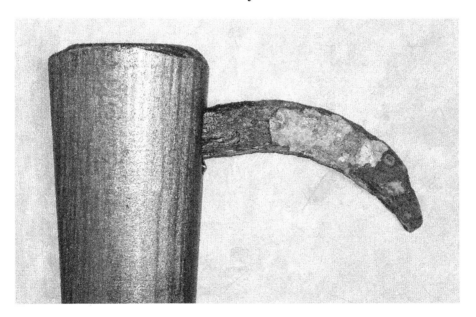

Saxon Mattock in use (Bayeaux Tapestry)

The battlefield area was large and the area of English pursuit of the fleeing Norse – Irish - Scottish army even larger, and it likely extended northwards into the Prenton and Tranmere areas and westwards towards and past Thingwall (see section 3 for a detailed analysis). Perhaps there were other weapon collection sites? More detailed analysis of the composition of weapon types found may tell us more but the rough numbers do suggest that the armies engaged were large as the chronicles tell us: in the tens of thousands. Is this also the location where the victorious Mercians camped, on sloping dry ground with a good water source, just south of the field of carnage and its thousands of rotting corpses?

It has been suggested that after the battle the Mercians not only pursued the invaders but also rooted out Anlaf sympathisers among the local Viking settlers and 'dealt' with them (see section 3). Perhaps the Mercian camp at Poulton Lancelyn was active for weeks? Was the whole Wirral area ethnically cleansed, with many Norse settlers killed or moved south to Chester where in the coming years a large Viking trading community would emerge?

Was this also the forward camp where, according to Egil the Skald, the Norse envoys were fooled into delaying battle by rows of empty Mercian tents set along the ridge, giving time for King Aethelstan to bring up his main army from Chester? Egil's Saga tells us the English tents

'were so high no one could see over them to find out whether they were many or a few rows deep.'

If you stand at the weapon recovery site centre looking up to the ridge line this is still the situation. Although the 'tent stratagem' is often rejected as a typical skaldic device it is remarkably consistent with the local landscape. Perhaps we have here a surviving eyewitness account.

(Egil buried his brother by 'Vina's green bank' just half a mile to the north... or did he make *this* up too? See section 3). But later that first battle day Egil tells us that a Viking probing group, suspecting a trick, attacked the Mercian camp and were routed, fleeing north back to their camp near Storeton. Perhaps a lot more material remains in the north fields, next to J4 of the M53. This is speculative of course but we may conclude that this impressive material find, finally, provides the smoking gun of Brunanburh.

Poulton Lancelyn is north of the often presumed boundary between the Saxon settlements to the south and the Norse / Irish lands at the time of Brunanburh. To the east of Poulton the area of Bromborough was assumed to be Saxon despite many Norse names on the land. Those names stretch between the current Bromborough village and Poulton Hall and there is an ancient pathway across the Dibbin valley. (See Appendix 2 for a longer discussion of Norse names distribution on Wirral). Was there also a Norse or mixed settlement at Poulton and Spital?

The author's house stands just below the ridge line not far from the Mercian metal recovery camp site discussed above. There was ample room along that ridge along to Poulton Hall for Aethelstan's large army to camp, perhaps for some time, while the local Viking settlers were screened for loyalty.

Hopefully official protection is being sought for the area before this nationally important site is identified publically and the find results formally published. Wirral Archaeology stress that there is much more work to do even in the immediate area and the main battle area is large. An area from Brimstage to Storeton, Higher Bebington, Brakenwood and Poulton Lancelyn south to Poulton Hall, west to Clatterbridge and back to Brimstage, is implicated. The fact that so much material from the battle is still here, some distance from its presumed centre, strongly suggests that much may remain *in situ* across the battlefield. The case for giving physical protection to this whole area from would be looters and nighthawks should be obvious to Wirral Council which has responsibility in the matter. However the council neglect of important **listed** ancient sites like Overchurch is not encouraging.

The only good news is that computer controlled, low light security cameras are both effective and affordable and now local watch groups are being organized in the area. Many local people are aware of the situation and will keep an eye out for rogue lights on the fields.

Overall there is sufficient evidence now to protect this whole area 'Round Brunanburh' from the council proposed, green belt release for housing development along the M53 corridor as part of the Wirral Local Plan. This includes both the Local Plan **option 2B 'Urban extensions' and option 2A 'Dispersed green belt release' developments. Such developments would be reckless, illegal, cultural vandalism.** Despite 1,100 years of farming and the driving of the M53 through the eastern part of the battlefield, much of the probable battle area, and much material from the battle may remain, including several suspected mass grave sites and camps. The probable Norse army escape routes, particularly to the west, and northwest over open farm land, should also be explored and protected.

Much of mid-Wirral is definitely implicated in the Brunanburh story. Much of this land is owned by Leverhulme Estates who have recently published a propaganda 'Vision' for building 'beautiful' garden villages in this area of Green Belt agricultural land. Given the current development on the ancient Storeton Village site (Anlaf's camp), around Storeton Hall, we can expect a flood of large luxury houses. The distorted 'pitch' is that William Lever built the iconic Port Sunlight workers village under a similar enlightened 'Vision. Actually Billy built his village right next to his soap factory on recovered marsh land and filled in muddy inlets of the River Dibbin north of Bromborough Pool. This was not Green Belt land but wasteland, and Billy wanted his workers living just ten minutes walk from his factory (not thirty minutes away along dangerous, congested roads, driving polluting 'four by fours' and SUVs. That is the nightmare vision implied by Leverhulme Estates and its new garden villages. WMBC, by contrast, agrees with Billy Lever and will *aim* to build new housing near to where the jobs are and will be, if we are lucky: to the east on brown field land.)

Section 3   Defining the Possible Extended Battlefield Area

'Round Brunanburh they broke the shield wall,
These sons of Edward with their well forged swords...'

The Anglo-Saxon Chronicle

Nearly 1,100 years have passed since Brunanburh and much has changed in England. However toponyms related to great events can survive, as can local legends. Sometimes meaningful names are still there in plain sight and should be sought out, in our case by considering Old English, Old Norse, local dialects and the Celtic languages of Britain (3,4,5,6,10,11,12,14,19,23,24,25,26,27,28). Below we examine several local names and show how they can be linked to names in the chronicles and sagas which discuss Brunanburh. Some links such as current river names seem very strong, followed by traditional local wood and tithe field names, often in clusters. **Many of the names relate to conflict, warrior names, weapons and graves.** Others are more tentative suggestions but worthy of further investigation. Overall, the picture is surprisingly suggestive.

Harding also mentions a place name in the Bromborough parish which should first be considered briefly: Brimston or Brimstone. Brimstone is of course an old name for sulphur but no deposits are known in Wirral. However Brynstan may be OE since brin is from brinnen, 'to burn'. (In German we also have brennen, 'to burn'). In Middle English various other forms *of some interest* emerged from the dictionary: brem, brom, brun, bron...To see brem, brom and brun together is striking. It is also interesting that in Old German brem also means to rage or roar. We could read the name as brinstan, burning stone, or as bremstan, raging stone. A raging stone would be a good memorial marker name for a battle site. The Merseyside HER website also mentions the name Bremesbyrig and Professor Livingston provides a list of burhs and fortified sites established (or rebuilt) by Aethelfeda in the early 10th century (34). We mentioned Runcorn, Chester and Eddisbury but another burh, of unknown location, was Bremesburh / Bremesbyrig in 910 (or 909, or 912 in various places). Could this have been Brimstage? However 'byrig' is simply the plural of 'burh'. Could byrig refer to the two *refortified* burh sites, Brimstage and Poulton Hall which we have already suggested? Other suggestions have been Bromsgrove (and earlier Bromsgraf) and Bromesberrow / Bremesberry. These sites may instead be simply Breme's burial sites, not burhs.

Close by Junction 4 is Umberstone Covert: covert of the shadow stone. It is also interesting that early 19th century maps show the ancient, 'Neston Cross' on the Old Clatterbridge Road just south of Brackenwood and west of Poulton Lancelyn. The enclave of 'Hargrave – Little Neston' is over a mile to the south. Did this cross commemorate the battle site? In 1874 remains of four early crosses were found at the church of St. Mary & St. Helen in Neston. The largely secular images suggested a Norse rather than Saxon origin. Fragment 5; face C, showed two horsemen, with lances, in combat (19). An upper fragment shows two men in combat with short swords (shown opposite). In reconstructions the shaft is topped with a Christian cross in a circular enclosure. Did this cross also commemorate the famous Battle of Brunanburh? Did it stand originally at Clatterbridge next to the battle site?

Egil's Saga and other later sources describe the great battle of Vinheidi which is generally identified with Brunanburh. Egil and his brother were certainly in the employment of Aethelstan in the right period. The interesting question is: can we identify any local place names related to Vinheidi? The battlefield of Brunanburh may well have stretched from Storeton and Higher Bebington, southwards through Brackenwood and Clatterbridge (the presumed centre) and Poulton Lancelyn as far south as the possible stronghold at Poulton Hall. If Brimstage was the main Saxon burh, and in use at the time, conflict could have stretched from there, eastwards through Lower Bebington and Spital to modern Bromborough Pool on the Mersey banks, another suggested strongpoint (see below).

3.1   The Northern Battle Area: Around Storeton

Local tradition points to some interesting names. To the west of Mount Road, Storeton Woods slope down westwards and then open onto several large fields cut by a few old, deep and narrow lanes.

We have Red Hill Road and Rest Hill Road and around it an area known as 'Battlefields'. Just to the west of Battlefields the author notes two large, adjacent fields on the 1839 tithe map, 92 & 95: Bowman meadow and Bowman (22). These could be surnames of course. However, the nearby land has conventional land names such as marsh hey, town yard, rye wood, and intack, in Old Norse, enclosure. Do we have here bowman as in archer, another battle memory? There is one other curious name nearby worth attention: 'Wet Reins'. Reins is 12th century Anglo-Norman with the familiar meaning : horse reins. But in ON we also have raun meaning test, trial; rena to diminish; renna means 'to put to flight'. We should also note one of several terms or kennings in Old Norse, for battlefield : vaettfang, pronounced wetfang. Fang means a contest in OE. In fact vaetta means to wet, to stain. We also have vaetr, a spirit or ghost. This makes vaettfang a typical poetic kenning for a battlefield: a 'wet contest', in this case of blood; a (blood) stained contest; a contest of spirits (souls?). Wet raun has the same meaning. Wet renna would mean a (blood) stained flight. Or could our Wet Reins, blood stained reins, record a cavalry battle, or at least the pursuit of fleeing Norsemen by Mercian cavalry after the main battle? Fangen means to capture in OE.

West of this area, the land rises again steeply to the sandstone ridge at Storeton village and we have 'Soldier's Hill'. Local tradition identifies the area as a battle (or camp) site but the age of these names is unknown. The author has always considered the high, open ground at Storeton a good place for an encampment...for a force coming from the north. There are many stories. A local man told me recently of visiting a farm house as a child and being shown a lance head and a skull...supposedly from the battle. One wonders how much material has been unofficially 'curated' locally over the centuries.

By coincidence, no doubt, Harding points to an interesting ancient name at Storeton by Soldier's Hill: Le Gremotehalland (date 1330) from the Old Norse grida = truce and mot = meeting, giving grida-mot (4). So we have the place of the meeting under a truce. A halland is a strip of field of a particular area. However 'hallr' also means a slope, hill, big stone, flat rock in ON.

The Storeton village ridge, rising from the low Rest Hill Road to the east, consists of a large natural sandstone platform, an excellent defensive position. ON 'hals' means a ridge or hill crest, a perfect description of the village. Could this have been a genuine memory of a pre-battle meeting place between the Saxons and the Norse-Irish?

Egil's Saga and other sources make it clear that such negotiations and even the physical limits of a battlefield could be pre-defined and agreed at such meetings. I will give reasons later as to why this area of Wirral was chosen for the battle. For completeness I also note ON haela, hero, giving us 'the place of the truce meeting of heroes', a very appropriate skaldic description!

Accepting Egil the Skald's battle description, Anlaf's forces were chased northwards from the main battle field, probably through Storeton, the probable Norse camp, and Prenton. We noted several conflict tithe fields on the presumed main battle site around Brimstage Road at Clatterbridge. Just south of Storeton in the vicinity of Keepers Lane, the Roman road line, we note other fields of interest. Just east of and adjacent to Keepers Lane we have the tithe fields Ox Pasture & New Hey (No. 35) and Two New Heys (No. 29). Recall that in ON, ox means axe. Also we saw that OI tua also means axe. We have renamed fields perhaps referring back to older names recording conflict here in the languages of the main Norse-Irish army. To the west of the Roman road line nearby, we have two Oxen Dough fields, Nos. 140 & 141. Again ON ox means axe. Also dugr means boldness, courageous, fearless and doegr means day. We could read fearless axes or day of the axes.

Adjacent to the old (medieval?) paved road known locally as Roman Road, on Prenton golf course, we had two tithe fields, 207 & 214, called Welsh Graves in 1839 (22). Now the Saxons called the remnant Celts of Wallasey (and elsewhere) 'welsh' which meant strangers. But it is true that Anlaf brought both Irish & Scots Celts and the Strathclyde Welsh of King Owain, including those from the north Wales coast, to Wirral. Are these grave names a genuine memory of Aethelstan's triumphant men catching and slaughtering the fleeing Celts and Norse? Close nearby we also have 'Greets' and 'Raw' fields. Greets in OI and of course in Scottish dialect, means to lament, weep, cry. In ON gratr also means lament.

The locals remember, were a mixture of old British (Celts), settled Norse – Irish farmers and some Saxons. Raw is also an unusual name for a field with no discernable farming connection. But raw in English has long meant red, inflamed, painful. However, was raw once roar: the noise of a crowd; a loud shout of anger? However note also ON, wal – rauvar, 'spoils taken from the slain' (in battle) so rauvar are spoils and in Norse v is pronounced w.

There are other ON field names in the area such as Copstige, where stigr means path, giving the copse (or corpse?) path. By Marsh Lane we have field no. 227, Tuvit. This is a personal name in Turkish which seems unlikely. Again in ON However tu may be tiu, ten. We saw that vaettfang was a battle with vaett meaning stain (of blood) but also vaetr (pronounced witr?) means spirit. We may have 'ten spirits' here but note in OI tua is an axe giving us 'axe spirits' or 'axe stains'. Just north west of Little Storeton we have plot 195, Faugh Hey. Faugh! still means to express disgust but in OI we have the famous battle cry 'Faugh A Ballagh', 'clear the way'. Nearby is the plot Galleons. This has the look of something alien translated or rendered into English. In ON we have galla, to scream. Was this plot once Gallaloons, the selion, the field, of screams? However gjalla is also a known kenning for the 'twang of a bowstring'. These fields are on a line from the battlefield towards Meols, the Viking port, and perhaps a chance of escape?

Storeton, the great farmstead in ON, has other associations worth mentioning which support the idea of long surviving, local traditions in the area. The present Storeton Hall was built in 1370 and was long the holding of the Stanleys. Professor Harding has suggested that the Hall was the site of the Green Chapel which features in the medieval poem, Sir Gawain and the Green Knight (4, 13), based on his geographical analysis and dialect mapping. In Middle English we have

'All the iles of Anglesey on lyft half he holdes
and fares over the fordes by the forlondes, over at the Holy Hede,
til he had eft bonk in the wyldernesse of Wyrale...'

Holy Hede is probably Hollywell, where stands the ancient shrine of St Winifred, like the Green Knight himself, decapitated and miraculously restored to life. The Wirral certainly appears prominently in the Gawain poem and dialect analysis shows a strong Norse presence along with Cheshire and Lancashire dialect words. Harding suggests that Sir John Stanley of Storeton Hall, brother of the Master Forrester of Wirral, wrote the poem. Others have suggested it was commissioned by another ancient, prominent landowning family, the Masseys. The author has looked into the Gawain Poet and his works and finds many strange features relating to ancient stone sites in the area (31). Mid-Wirral may have had a long history still respected at the time of Brunanburh which explains why the battled was located here. (See section 3). The point is, Storeton is an important site of ancient habitation and conflict. As of this writing, developers now have government permission (after appeal) to 'refurbish' the grade II listed Hall, insert 'flats' into it, and surround it with dozens of luxury houses, on the green belt, which will be visible for miles around. So much for heritage protection on Wirral. With the relaxation of national planning regulations in 2020 it is clear that more local and national heritage desecration is to come: the reason this book is being written now.

Harding also notes another Storeton location called Le Dedemonnes Greue (1323): The Deadmen's Wood (Grove). Did the battle also encompass Storeton Woods, where many fleeing Norsemen were hacked down by the triumphant Saxon host, as Egil describes? Perhaps, although in ON greue also means earl: maybe we have 'the deadmen of the earl' or 'the earl of deadmen', one of the seven Norse earls killed that day at Brunanburh. In ON grove is actually lundr.

On the edge of Storeton Woods, from Marsh Lane south to Red Hill Road are a dozen tithe fields (85 – 90; 62-68) named Wanton Dale. In ME and modern English wanton describes 'deliberate and unprovoked, cruel, vicious or violent action'. We also note ON vandr (pronounced wandr) which means evil, bad: hence wandrtun dale. This could relate to the slaughter of fleeing Norsemen (as seen from the viewpoint of the local Norse settlers). However it has also been noted that Wanton looks rather like Wendune, which is another name for our battle (8). This is not unreasonable but the main battle action was probably further south and south west.

According to local tradition Red Hill Road is so called because of the rivers of blood which flowed down it during the great battle. Note that in ON red is 'raudr' and bloodstained is 'rodinn'. It is interesting that in ON hraeddr means frightened and raeddoghe means fear. Also we have reidr in ON which means anger, wrath.

However, 'd' here is pronounced 'th' bringing us closer to the English wrath in speech. Did the name come from a written source or a verbal source? Only attachment to the road via a written source would give us 'Reidr Hill Road' or 'Red Hill Road'. This is a general problem with name interpretation. I also note ON areid which is a cavalry charge. Note that in old Cheshire dialect 'rute'

means to roar or bellow (related to the current, 'to root for', to shout support) which sounds like the OG, rote, red. So we would have the road of the roaring hill (12) to complement Clatterbrook, the raging, berserker, stream and Brackenwood, the clashing woods and Iveston, the archers' camp and Needwood, the wood of harm. More simply in 13th century and current English we have 'rout', a disorderly retreat, giving us Rout Hill Road. We can also legitimately read the 'rest' (ON) in Rest Hill Road as resting place, as in a grave, to lie dead. In ME reste means that which remains, the remnant. This is a curious set of conflict name coincidences (see below for more explanation).

Just north of Storeton, Anlaf's proposed fortified camp, on the old Marsh Lane stands Ethel's Covert. It was present on early 19th century OS maps but its age is unknown. I simply note that Ethel derives from the root Aethaele in OE, and Athal in ON, meaning noble, as in Aethelstan, the King of Mercia, Victor of Brunanburh.

Did he bury some of his noble dead there after the battle or did Anlaf have time to do so for his own nobles before he fled?Aethelstan lost two cousins in the battle : Aethelwine and Aelfwine. Their bodies are supposedly buried at Malmesbury (where Aethelstan was also later buried). But is Aethal's Covert where they fell? Or where other nobles fell? Remember, 'five kings and seven earls' fell at Brunanburh. Note: atall in ON, means fierce, terrible, giving alternatively, the wood of terror. The covert site still shows up well on the Lidar maps.

Ethel's Covert

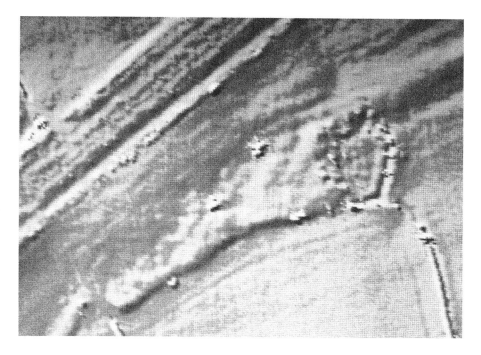

Of some interest is the elliptical bank / ditch at the north east corner of Ethel's Covert. It is about 80 ft long by 50 ft wide. A mass grave marker ? The Deadmen's Wood? Recall that just to the northwest, across Lever Causeway we noted tithe fields called 'Welsh Graves'.

According to Egil the Norse fled after the battle. The evidence suggests they certainly fled north and north westwards and Harding believes also westwards, past the Thing site, to the west coast at Dawpool and perhaps Meols. We noted earlier interesting field names near Whitehouse Lane west of Brimstage.

North from Little Storeton we note 'The Slangton & Pits' No. 24. In ON sla is to strike and slangva is hurt, throw so we could have the striking settlement. We should also note the ON slaga, a slayer.

Due north from Prenton takes us through modern Birkenhead, via the Arno, Claughton, Birkenhead Park, to the banks of Wallasey Pool. Just south of the Arno site we find 'Harner & Pits'.

ON harmr means sorrow. This is another obvious escape route, but difficult to track because of urbanization. However at Claughton we cross Ufaldi's Green which provided the kernel of the new park. Ufaldi was a major Norse landowner suggesting a significant Norse presence in the area.

Close to the medieval Blake Street line we have Big Suck Fields. In ON soekja meant attack. Yet again our path crosses an ancient standing stone site in the park and by the banks of Wallasey Pool we note two more. The interested reader should consult Appendix 5. On the old maps Lowfield Lane crosses the park very close to the estimated route of Blake Street, the last stretch of the eastern Roman road. Blake Street crosses the road line from Storeton at the Arno. Low has been read as lowe or hlaw, meaning burial mound and in the 19th century mounds called 'The Bonks' were still visible near the lane. On the road line we also have 'Trowster' possibly from OE, treow meaning faith, belief suggesting, perhaps recording a sacred site.

The Arno is interesting. The area has several arno tithe fields and a Roman coin hoard was found just to the east of the Blakestrete line through the site. It is usually assumed the area was named for a Norse settler called Arni so we obtain Arni's haugr, Arni's burial mound. However it is worth noting other ON words. 'Orn', or arn, and 'ari' mean eagle. (Less likely we note arr, unwary and oerr, mad, frantic). The possible occurrence of the name eagle on a Roman road line is interesting (and it may have happened again in Arrowe Park on the proposed western Roman road line. See below).

North east of Storeton on the borders of Higher Bebington near Mount Road, we note tithe field no.133, 'Bone Dust Field'. Perhaps this was a field treated regularly with bone meal? If so it was the only one in the wider area. Dust means dust in all the languages we have considered. But in Gaelic and northern dialect, dust is used figuratively to mean corpse, presumably in the sense of the Christian burial service: ashes to ashes and dust to dust. Adjacent we have several fields involving 'norridge'. We note that nar in ON is a corpse and nagrindr are the gates of the dead. Do we have corpse ridge, or corpse gate?

Our fields are on the direct escape route to Tranmere (Inlet and beach) from Storeton and to the eastern end of Wallasey Pool. On the way we note several interesting field names: Walley Hay, Wall Butts and Short Butts. In ON valr, 'walr', is a battle corpse. In OE butts initially meant a target and later an archery field, as well as the use of the head as a weapon.

Near the Tranmere pool we find four Yolk of Egg fields, the same name as we find by Poulton Hall (see section 3.3 for a detailed discussion). Yoke as a field name in OE was the area that a pair of oxen could plough in a day. Egg in OE and ON meant egg but in ON it was also an 'edge' and a common kenning for a sword and a battle, as in 'conflict of edges'.

3.2 Escape to the West from Storeton & Brimstage

A thorough examination of possible escape routes marked by skirmish or death related names on the land is worthwhile. To whet the appetite, just west of Barnston Road opposite the Wirral Thing site we note field no. 22, 'Two Loaves & Money Pits'. Nearby is 'Two loves' no. 25, 'Big Two Loaves no. 26 and 'Little Two Loves' no. 12. These tithe fields are due west of Storeton, the presumed Viking battle camp. When the shield wall broke the Norse might at first retreat northwards towards their camp.

A further defeat (or rout) might drive them west towards Norse centres at Thingwall, Irby, Thurstaston and Dawpool: Professor Harding's suggested port of the Thing (at the River Dee; his Dingesmere?). The money pits are most interesting...possibly local, Viking hoard sites? The names 'two loaves' and 'two loves' look like a later English take on foreign words. Tiu is ten in ON but nothing in ON accounts for 'loaves'. Since we are dealing with a mixed Norse – Irish population here perhaps Old Gaelic can help. The author notes the following words

tua = axe   tuaigh (verb), 'to chop with an axe'
lofa = rotten (as in ubh lofa , rotten egg)
lath = rutting of an animal (as in aimsir lath , rutting season); or in literary use, a kenning for warrior
leafa, a grammatical form of leamh (verb) = to render impotent;

leamh (adjective) = weak, impotent; when applied to a man = 'weak in combat'
leidr, leithr = hateful

The reader can no doubt see the obvious combinations of interest here:

tua lath   'axe warrior'
tuaigh leafa   'by axe chopped down or the weak in combat'
tuaigh lofa   'by axe made rotten'

The combination of 'money pits' at a clear conflict site next to the Thing site is striking. This location is also on two Norse army escape routes from Brunanburh: to Moels, northwest along the old Roman road line; to Dawpool, the port of the Thing on the Dee, due west.

While near Cross Hill (Thing) we note just to the east, The Folly, no. 1, on Prenton Brook, possibly from the Norman French folie, meaning madness, lunacy but also in earlier times, evil, wickedness. However in OI we have 'fail', faigh + ail, pronounced foil meaning a gain, a win. North east of Cross Hill we find Whelpers, no. 82 and Gala Pitts, no. 62. OE hwelp and ON hvelpr mean whelp: an impudent or reckless youth; offspring of a female dog or wolf or sometimes applied to a woman as in 'son of a bitch'. These terms are all somewhat derogatory. Also near Barnston Road we note Gala Pitts, no. 62. We met galla earlier at the Storeton battle site meaning scream in ON but also as gjalla, 'the twang of a bowstring'.
Below we will trace in detail a line of tithe fields marking a probable Norse 'fighting retreat' route from the battlefield centre to the coast at Dawpool . In doing so we cross the line of the conjectured old Roman road to Meols from Deva.

We repeat Figure B here, showing probable battlefield escape routes, for reader convenience. There is one further major clue worth exploring in relation to the west. The late Annals of Clonmacnoise (1627) talk of the battle taking place on the 'Plaines of Othlynn'. This has sometimes been read as 'Odlynn' or 'Ochlynn'. Od or Oc supposedly imply 'up to'. (We also have 'odr' which means frenzied, raging, berserk, divine madness but we also note the Norse minor god, Od, the first, randy, husband of the goddess Freya).

We could also read Ot Hlynn but Hlin in Norse mythology is goddess of compassion: bringer of comfort, reliever of grief, to mourners. Poetically we have the Plains of Compassion, a very skaldic but also Christian construct for a field of death.

Of course in the Celtic languages we have in OW, llyn, a lake and in Gaelic, linn a pool. In OE lynn is variously a pool, a lake, a stream or a deep section of a river. So we may have plains 'up to' or bordering a river or pool. Or as likely, the plains of the frenzied, raging, berserker, river. We have the same meaning here as we suggested for Clatterbrook. We also note another possibility if the Irish informants were Norsemen.

Afl in ON means might, strength, so we have the Plains of the River of Might, also a reasonable name for a field of battle. Curiously otti in ON is fear so Othlynn is also readable as 'river of fear'.

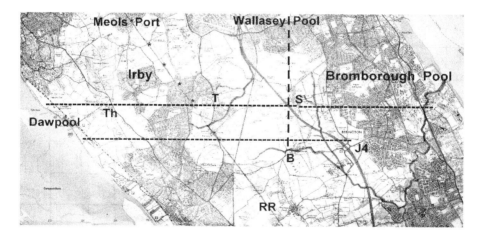

This is all consistent with Egil's description of the battle area. **It is also said that Prenton Brook to the west of Brimstage was once known as the Athlyn locally (8).**

The brook valley possibly forms a natural western boundary for our battlefield with the Wirral Thing site at Cross Hill just a few hundred yards to its west. The Norse settlers looking east to the main battlefield might well name it for their local river, the Plains of

Athlyn, with the survivors later reaching Ireland and giving this toponym for the battle to the Irish clerics and chroniclers.

Is there anything of interest in the tithe fields this far west in the latitude of Brimstage? Possibly. ¾ mile due west of Brimstage is Whitehouse Lane and Whitehouse Farm. We noted that in ON vitr is white, viti is misfortune, punishment and hauss is a skull. But we noted earlier that vaett, pronounced white, appears in vaettfang, another kenning for battle, where vaet can be a stain (as of blood) but also a spirit, soul. If we go west across Barnston Road we enter Whitfield Meadows no. 175 and Whitfields no. 177 continuing the 'vaett' theme (Note also Big White Hey no. 155, east of Pensby Road). This string of vaett names is on a line from Brimstage to Dawpool on the coast. Coincidence perhaps, but ½ mile northwest of Brimstage, towards Prenton Brook, are several large fields called Roundsills (nos. 39 to 43 and 73, 77). No. 134 nearby is called Ransel. Now in ON rond is one name for a shield and in ON and OE syll is a threshold, a doorway. If we were in skaldic mood we might be describing a door, a break, in a shield wall. We also have Ransel. In ME, ransel is a beating and in northern dialect means to ransack, steal (loot?). These fields are just to the south west of the Oxen Dough, axes of courage, tithe fields.

Just to the east of Roundsills and west of Brimstage Village are two fields called Leavelands (N0. 56, 62). In ON leifa also means leave but also 'abandon, to leave after death'. We also noted earlier leita, attack, assault and Leidr, pronounced 'leithr' meaning hateful.In OI we also have leafa meaning to make impotent but also applied to a man, weak in combat. Just west of Ley Farm is another Clatterbridge; another bridge across a stream on the escape route, focusing conflict at a pinch point? A hundred yards north of Ransel are the buildings of Ley Farm. Surprisingly this is one of only 3 Ley farm place names in Cheshire. Ley means field in early English and occurs frequently in the south. However in ON lae (possibly pronounced lie) means harm, destruction, misfortune. We may have a set of local memories here of violent events and a fighting retreat of the Norsemen...on the western edge of the Plaines of Othlynn.

Interestingly west of Ley Farm near the Prenton Brook (Athlyn) we also note no. 47 and 101, Big Back Grave and Little Back Grave.

Recall that grafa means to dig, bury in ON. In Cheshire dialect graft is 'the depth of a spade' in digging and intriguingly, graith means riches. Do these names mark a 'mass' grave site following a serious western skirmish? (For completeness note ON bak means back and bacraut is arsehole). We should also note on the northern boundary of Little Back Grave a circular earthwork surrounding a mound on the oldest maps. This could be of any date from the Neolithic onwards to our battle times. It is now ploughed away.

Half way along and north of Whitehouse Lane we note tithe fields 65, 66, 67, Batty Grounds. Is this a corruption of Battle Grounds? By Batty Grounds we have the strange, alien, name Affghan Meadow. After some searching I found Athghoin in OI. As a verbal noun it means 'further wound'. As a verb it means 'to rewound'. 'Roundsills', discussed earlier, is just to the north of this field cluster and in between we have 'Ramsdale' no. 61 and 'Little Ramsdale' no. 60. Harding listed these two names in his general survey of Norse toponyms and translated them as 'Hrafns Dalr' - Ravens Dale - Valley of the Ravens (4). The author was immediately taken back to the description of the Brunanburh battlefield in the Anglo Saxon Chronicle.

> 'They left behind the corpses for the dark
> Black coated raven, horny beaked, to enjoy'

In fact the raven is also called in ON: valgammar – (battle) corpse vulture; valgunnar – falcon of battle; even valpidurr – carnage grouse. The name may indeed record a conflict here.

Just west of Batty Grounds, across Barnston Road is Carnsdale Farm. This appears to be the site of the lost Norse settlement of Haby. In OI, OE, OW and Scots Gaelic carn is a cairn, burial mound or barrow. In NF carn is of course flesh. Dead flesh perhaps? We also still have tithe fields Haby House no. 137 and Haby Kiln no. 136. Harding interprets Haby as ha – byr with ha being high in ON. However we also have ON haer meaning army. Do we have Haer – byr, the army settlement, a local strongpoint? In written form this is close to Haby. In spoken form (by a Norseman) it would be more like Hirby, with ae pronounced as a hard i giving Higherby taking us back to ha. However Haby was not on a hill top.

The farm is at ~60 ms elevation, the land to the east at ~50ms and the land nearby to the west, the Heswall Ridge is at ~100 ms. I suggest Ha in Haby is therefore more likely to be Haer- army.

Also west of Barnston Road on Gill Lane we have plots 24 and 25, Griffins Head. Griffin is still a common Irish name, originally griobh, griofa meaning 'griffin like', fierce. In ME griffin was likewise a nickname for 'a dangerous or fierce person'. Was something suitably marshal found on Gills Lane? A helm, perhaps? In ON poetry a head is a 'helm – stub'.

To the north, old paths and lanes lead westwards from Little Storeton through Landican and across Arrowe Park to the western Roman road. Near the first village we first find Faugh Hey (OI battle cry, 'Clear the Way') noted earlier and then Hasty Hey. Hasty has the old meaning, hurried, hot tempered. Approaching Landican on Landican Lane we have no. 141 'Hooks' and 144 'Sour meadow'. We met these names before on Brimstage Road near the battle field centre. In ON hogg means blow, execute or behead. But we also noted ME, Old Saxon, ON haukr and hauk, a hawk but also 'a young and brave man'. Sarr means wounded and soera, a wound. Nearby is plot no. 113, Nostage. In OI nos is used in literature as fame, renown. In OI staca is support, ON stakkr is a pile or pillar and in ME stache is a stage. A monument? Also at Landican we have plot 81, Three Nooks. But OE hnoc is a hook, or bent implement and in Norse dialect nok has the same meaning. Possibly indicating weapon finds?
 By Old Hall Farm on a tributary of Prenton Brook, we have the striking 'Dig Meat', no. 145. This has the look of a foreign name rendered into an English phrase. In ON we have digr, big, thick, deep, and meida, with d pronounced 'th' giving meathr which means to maim, injure. This gives us the field of 'big (or deep) injury'. However the full name could be OI. Dige is a drain outlet. Meata is craven, cowardly and meath is failure. Perhaps there was a skirmish here with the losers thrown into the stream. But in ON dugr is courage, boldness giving us 'the courageous wounded'.

On Arrowe Park Road at Landican Cemetery we cross Wanton Dale which we also met near Storeton Woods: wanton, once meaning unwarranted, vicious and violent action.

A route west across Arrowe Park leads over a large standing stone site to Wharton's Arrowe field with interesting rectangular crop marks.

The proposed western Roman road line drawn from Meols (Dove Point) Roman 'port' site to Chester North Gate passes through this tithe field. Arrowe Park is yet another ancient stones site which we cross on escape routes near Roman roads (30, 31). The name Arrowe is usually interpreted as a shieling, from ON erg, but elsewhere Harding also translates Harrowe as ON, harrhaugr, higher burial mound or even OE hearg, heathen temple. Simple 'arrow' at the park was presumably considered unlikely… given one was unaware of the grave and conflict names in the immediate area associated with two possible major battlefield escape routes.

Two other ON names should be mentioned in the context of the medieval poem concerning Wirral, Sir Gawain and the Green Knight, which we touched on earlier, if only because of links to fascinating Celtic regional folklore (31). The names are ON 'ari' and 'orn'(from proto-Germanic 'aro') , pronounced arn, meaning eagle. OW eryr is also eagle. Curiously ON 'or' is an arrow compared with 'orn', eagle. One can see that given the similarity of names and meanings orn / arn could could morph into or / ar, arrow. If we take Harding's reading of owe as haugr, burial mound, we get arhaugr or arrowe. (Note also ON arr, unwary and oerr, mad, frantic).

Let's look at the regional folklore in this light. Sir Gawain originated in Welsh mythology as Gwalchmai, 'The Hawk of May'. He comes to the Wirral (Cilgwri) on a quest to seek out Mabon, the hunter and ancient solar god. His party encounters magical animals whom they question. One is the Eagle of Kingdoms who does not remember Mabon despite his magically long life. He tells them

'I came here long ago and when I first came, *I stood on a great stone and from its top I would peck at the whirling stars at night.* But now my talons have worn it away to the small stone, a hand's breadth high, on which I stand.'

The sense of deep time is palpable.

It is interesting to note that another bird of prey, the hawk, is a solar symbol in several cultures. In the Dendera Planisphere of Egypt the summer solstice is represented by a hawk standing on a stone pillar. But Gwalchmai is also a hawk and other tales confirm him as a solar deity who, in some tales, is buried in Wirral. It is tempting to see here a memory, or rationalization of, some great observational standing stone site, which Arrowe Park was, where adepts studied the movements of the sun and stars. Perhaps it was once the Arowe, the Eagle grave / heathen temple site. There is another well known Norse folklore element which may have reinforced the eagle / grave name assignment here. The Norse stories record the 'Hraesvelgr', the corpse eater, the giant who takes the form of an eagle to consume the unworthy battle dead. Curiously the eagle hosts a symbiotic hawk which perches between his eyes.

It is interesting also that the Aro, Eagle site, overlaps the Roman road and a possible settlement there indicated by the crop marks. An Aquila was of course the Roman military standard and sometimes applied as a place name in the empire. There is also an astronomical connection here. Aquilo is the north wind and aquilonaris is northern. An alternative name clearly highlights the astronomical origin of Latin 'north' terms: septentrio means northern region from septentriones, the seven polar stars of the north. It is curious that our proposed Roman road sits adjacent to an ancient standing stone, calendrical observation site. We seem to have a number of overlapping name elements which fit what is on the ground. There is another site adjacent to the Blakestrete, proposed eastern Roman road with a possibly related name: The Arno (see section 3.1).

There are few signs of possible conflict north of this western escape line but at nearby Arrowebrook Farm and the tithe field, Wall Gutter. For wall we could read ON valr, pronounced walr, meaning a 'corpse fallen in battle'. This would give corpse gutter. A gutter could be a large field drain but nothing is visible on the largest scale maps. However in ON gudr is another name for battle. Curiously the field also hosts White Cottages but ON vaett , pronounced white, means stain, and vaettfang means battle field, the stain here being of blood.

We noted that vaetr means spirit. Wall Gutter is just a few hundred yards from the confirmed Roman road line west of Greasby Copse. There we find Great Loons, a tithe field of unexceptional size. It may be that great is actually OS grata or OE gretan and northern dialect greet, meaning weep, lament, which we met on the main battle site.

These field names on *a western, battle escape route* encourage us to look further west along the proposed southern route from Storeton. On the route to Thingwall we noted Big and Little Back Grave east of Storeton lane and just north, Shocking Dale at Barnston by Cross Hill and to the west, Griffin Head. On Station road just east of Cross Hill we find Crewny Croft and Crewny Dale. ME Crewe means 'a body of soldiers','reinforcements'. We also note nearby by Cross Hill, another Folley, a Breach Hay and Bleak Loons. The due west 'escape' route from Storeton to Dawpool, having passed the Thing, now crosses the built up areas of Pensby. However we can still trace the route on the early 19th century tithe maps.

South of Thingwall Road (east of Harrock Wood) we note 'Little White Greaves' no. 122 and 'Big White Graves' no. 127. We have noted several times that in ON vaett and vaet would be pronounced white by the local Norse and that vaett is a stain (of blood) and vaettfang is a battle while vaetr is a spirit. We also noted ON grafa, dig, bury. The reader may agree by now that reading these names as stained (with blood) graves or battle graves is not too fanciful. We may have more significant conflict grave sites here. It may not be a coincidence that the proposed Roman road passes along the boundary between these two grave tithe fields providing an escape north to Meols.

In the unbuilt area east of Harrock Wood, are several large fields called Autons or Antons (nos. 123, 125, 139, 142, 143). The name seemed unusual. Auton or Aughton is a very old name derived from Actuna or Ac-tun (in the Domesday Book of 1086) meaning the 'Place of the Oak'. Such sites were local meeting or assembly places, the equivalent of a council or moot (or Thing). As such the site may predate the Norse, Saxon and Roman occupations. The oak was sacred to the Iron Age Druids of Britain. Druid means 'man of the oak'. Such sites were still revered even in Christian times.

By accident the author discovered a certain large scale OS map which includes a set of standing stones adjacent to the Autons fields and south of Harrock Wood, which like those at Needwood Farm, involve interesting geometrical properties and calendrical horizon alignments. These stones may be Neolithic and are explored in Appendix 4. A late prehistoric site with a later Romano-British farmstead has been excavated at Irby village and there is reputedly good evidence there for site occupation from the Bronze Age to the Iron Age (29). The names in this area are repeatedly interesting.

Harrock is a known Anglo-Saxon name but may derive from the ON name, Eirikr. The early form of OE Harrock was Heirick but this means 'old oak wood' which seems to confirm the Autons, Antons, oak interpretation. Orrick similarly means an old oak tree.

Irby – Harrock Wood LIDAR Map: Green Belt Site SP060

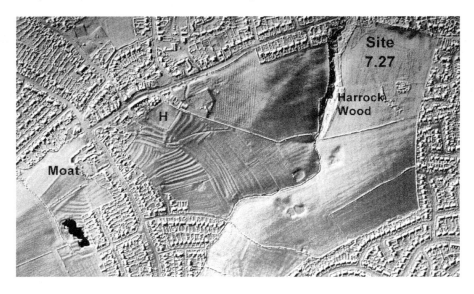

However there is also the Norman French Herec le fils Lac.
I mention this because Herec was slain by fellow knight of the round table, Sir Gawain, who famously came to 'the Wilderness of Wirral'. Irby, Ira - byr itself is accepted to indicate a Norse – Irish settlement (4). Immediately south of the village are several tithe fields called Heskeths (nos. 102, 103, 145, 146). This is accepted as hesta-skeidr: horse race field (4) where the d is pronounced th.

Just north of the Hesketh is a tithe field called 'Wet Reans', no. 101(see H on the Lidar Map above). We met a very similar name near Storeton on the northern margin of the battlefield : 'Wet Reins' with reins possibly relating to horse reins (cavalry?) and Wet construed as vaett (stain of blood) from vaettfang, battle or vaetr, spirit. Was Wet Reans, next to the Hesketh, the site of a skirmish here between the Norse troops retreating to the coast and Athelstan's pursuing cavalry? We noted at Storeton that ON renna means 'to put to flight' and raun is a test or trial. I note also the ON word, skoedan, 'skeethan', meaning hostile... Hesta skoedan, hostile horses?

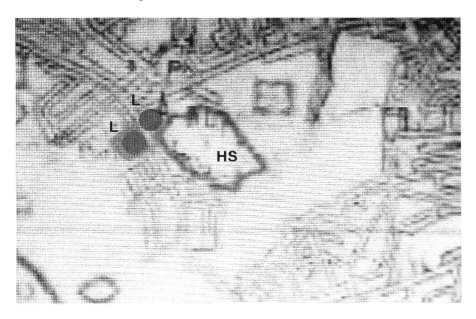

Note also on the Lidar map of Irby, the remarkably well preserved medieval field, ridge and furrow features, in the west (and again south of Irby Hall). These are the best preserved early fields on Wirral. The Hesketh area is recognised as a site of unusual heritage significance on the draft Local Plan, Sustainability Appraisal 'Historic Environment Map'. HS above, marks the area recorded as a Selected Heritage for Natural England Site (SHINE). Wirral has only 5 such sites, most much smaller. The circular symbols marked L are listed buildings. Are there other major clues? Perhaps. Immediately across Irby Road we have the ancient moated enclosure at Irby Hall alongside the old footpath to Thurstaston in the west.

Just south of Irby Hall we find three tithe fields called 'Greets' nos. 130, 148, 151. We met 'greets' before near the Storeton northern battlefield surrounded by conflict names. OE gretan and Old Swedish grata mean to weep or lament and in northern British dialects we have greet, still meaning, to cry.

At this point, as we approach the current Telegraph Road from the east, we need to consider points of access to the beaches adjacent to the Dawpool channel, Harding's proposed 'port' of the Wirral Thing. There are three. In the north there is an old farm path from Norse Thurstaston leading west to a gap in the low cliffs (At the Dee Sailing Club. On this path we have Flock Loons plot no. 11. In ON flokkr is 'a body of men'. Nearer Thurstaston we have The Nooks and Cinders. Considering Nooks we note ON hnuka, meaning to cower. The OE nook once meant safe haven, hideout, a rather similar idea.

The large sandstone blocks of a long 18th century quay exploiting the, then deep, Dawpool can still be seen) and a long stone causeway (of unknown age) leads out from the club to the Dawpool. This location is due west of the Thing site and Storeton. In the centre there is a deep valley (by tithe field 'Dawpool Meadow') in the high cliffs leading down to Shore Cottage. Half a kilometre to the south we have Tinkers Dale at the end of an old farm path from Thurstaston. This location on the high cliffs is the site of a lost Norse settlement called Stromby on early maps: the farmstead by the stream (4). Thirty years ago sandstone foundations still sat on the cliff edge there. Stromby is due west of Brackenwood and Brimstage. Troops escaping west to the coast from Brunanburh would likely head for this narrow band of Dee coastline (According to Harding, the AS Chronicle's Dingesmere).

On the coast we note 'Yaunsley' but jarn, 'yarn' in ON means weapon, giving a weapon field. Adjacent, are three fields called 'Harrow Hey'. Harrow, applied to a person means to harass, distress, cause pain to, alarm.

East of here we find three fields called 'Pike Hay' nos. 30, 33, 35 and 'Little Pike Hay' no. 32. At Stromby we also have 'Pike Field' no. 42.

We recall finding Pike fields in the proposed main battlefield area just north and south of Brimstage. The thrusting spear was a primary Norse weapon. Perhaps there was a final skirmish with the Mercians here, on the Dee coast. Tracking eastwards from here we cross the high point of Poll Hill in Heswall where a burial mound once stood. This was the centre of another, extended standing stone site.
Going eastwards again we find ourselves back at the series of Whitfield tithe fields and across the railway, at Whitehouse Lane and Batty Fields. Where the Roman road crosses this lane and Brimstage Road we note several 'Slaket Hey' fields. These align with the Roman road line. The word slaket is interesting. In ON sla or slaga is to strike, smite and kot with o pronounced e or u, meaning flesh.

The line from the coast to the Roman road follows old paths which are even clearer to the east, crossing the eastern Roman road via other conflict name fields, such as three fields called the 'Dig lakes' (ON 'dugr', fearlessness, courage; ON 'la' is blood; ON 'lag' is stab, thrust) and then we have 'Pikes' at Clatterbridge. East from there runs an ancient green lane past our Alleloons weapon recovery camp at Poulton Lancelyn and over Vineyard Farm (Vinagarda?) to Bromborough Village. It seems more than a coincidence that this path joins the Vinagarda / Poulton Hall burh site across the eastern Roman road to the western Roman road and a line of conflict sites to the west coast (see the battlefield / escape route map on page 85).

East from Bromborough takes us to Wargraves and the Mersey banks. A little further south than Poulton Hall, on a line westwards, conflict field names disappear. There is also no sign of action on the proposed western Roman road south of this line. Did it exist at this time in the west?
The proposed western and eastern roads are only one and a half miles apart at this point and converging to the south. North of the line, the western Roman road appears to see escape route action as far north as Greasby.

3.3   South of the Main Battlefield

Now we should turn to the important area south and south east of the presumed battle centre since we already have a major Mercian camp

site there and the possible origin of the alternative battle name : Vinheidr. Despite all the earlier tantalising geographical material, evidence for the alternative battle name, Vinheidi would be definitive. The author has found only one highly suggestive location so far near our proposed Mercian weapon recovery site. At Poulton Lancelyn just north of the ancient Hall, lies Vineyard Farm .
The author attempted to discover the origin of 'Vineyard Farm' without success. Was it a fancy of the land owner or did it perhaps reflect memories of a time when vines *were* grown in Britain?

The high ridge at Poulton Lancelyn slopes significantly to the south southwest which first drew the author's attention to its calendrical observatory potential during the Late Neolithic and Bronze Ages. It is the ideal site on Wirral for observation of the winter solstice sunset using Clwyd Range hill notches. This alone deserves field investigation. The site is also linked astronomically to the Neolithic Calderstones passage grave in Liverpool (18). Given the right climate Vineyard Farm looks like an obvious vineyard candidate, but when?

It is proposed that the Roman Road from Deva to Wallasey Pool ran northwards just across the Clatterbrook valley and that Romano-British farms existed at Storeton (the 'Great Farmstead' in Old Norse) and probably also at Poulton Lancelyn (8). During the Roman climate optimum northern Europe was certainly considerably warmer than today and other English vineyards are known. Research has identified the sites of seven Romano-British vineyards with 4 in Northamptonshire, 1 in Buckinghamshire, 1 in Cambridgeshire and 1 in Lincolnshire (32). The south and east feature strongly here because of higher temperatures and lower rainfall, particularly in Northamptonshire. The eastern drier climate would reduce the problem of fungal vine infections. The west coast with prevailing Atlantic weather may have been too damp (see below). Scirard Lancelyn Green, whose family held the land for several centuries, has confirmed that the farm name is very old and tradition posits an actual vineyard site.
There is another dating possibility: the Medieval Climate Maximum, between 900 and 1250 AD, when the Scandinavian expansion took them to Greenland and Vinland as well as Ireland, the Wirral, Lancashire and Northumbria.

Some vineyards are documented from the eighth century but these are associated with monasteries and the supply of sacramental wine. In 1086 the Domesday Book which covered property and assets up to the River Tees, reported ~45 vineyards (42 definite) all in south east England, as in Roman times (33). All lie below a line from Ely (in Cambridgeshire) to Gloucestershire. It appears the English wine industry was later affected by the linking of the English Crown to Aquitaine in 1152, giving wide access to the superior product of the vineyards of Bordeaux. Later came the Black Death, climatic deterioration into the Little Ice Age and Henry VIII's dissolution of the monasteries. A vineyard at Poulton is unlikely at any time, based on the historical evidence. So where did the name come from?

Vineyard in Old Norse is Vingardr. As usual there are other etymological possibilities but they seem to be self-supporting in an interesting way. In Egil's Saga it is generally agreed that the warrior skald is describing the battle we know as Brunanburh. Egil uses three names to describe the area of the battle: Vinheidi (or Vinheidr); Vinuskogar; and a river, Vina. Heidi and heidar mean 'heath'. Professor Harding and others place the centre of the probably wide ranging battle at Spittle Heath, ½ mile north of Vineyard Farm. We have 'Vina heath' on this reading. Skogar means woods or forest so Vinuskogar is read as 'Vina woods'. These seem to be legitimate place names in principle but there are complications as usual. The river or stream at (or near) the battle site is 'Vina', again apparently relating to vine. Was Vina the Clatterbrook? Clatter in Old English and Norse refers of course to loud noise, from OE clatr and ON klattra : 'a noisy commotion, as of hard objects striking rapidly against each other', to clash, clang, slam, thud.

Similarly in Old Norse poetry the word 'hjaldr' literally means 'noise, tumult' but is often used poetically to mean 'battle'. Even more interesting, klaka in ON means to dispute. Klettr is a crag but there are none visible on the Clatterbrook. There are crags along lower Dibbinsdale, but far from the presumed battle centre.

The northern Clatterbrook is minor although its borders and those of related streams may have been marshy. Was the river described, our Vina, indeed the Clatterbrook and the Dibbin?

We noted earlier that from Brimstage eastwards we still have a feeder stream in a deep cut in the landscape which joins the deep, southern Clatterbrook and Dibbin valleys and ultimately stretches all the way around Poulton Lancelyn and Poulton Hall. However at Poulton Lancelyn there are also several permanent natural meres and more temporary lakes in winter.

The North Field at Vineyard Farm in 2015

The area east of Brimstage and part of Dibbinsdale are still flood risk areas. Just south west of the Hall is Raby Mere, which at almost a third of a mile long, is the largest mere on Wirral which lakes explain 'Poulton' and relate to lynn, etc.

Probably the Brimstage stream ditch – Clatterbrook - Dibbin valley line marked the actual southern boundary of the 'Plaines of Othlynn' but the raging, berserker, river of fear itself was the Clatterbrook at the northern edge of Poulton near Needwood (The Wood of Harm): a stream named not for its marshy, minor flow, but for the great and deadly conflict there.

It is tempting to see these names in relation to the Battle of Brunanburh; see below. Vineyard Farm is surrounded to the west and south by the deep valley of the southern Clatterbrook and to the east by the deep valley of the Dibbin. **If the Clatterbrook and Dibbin were once the Vina, the farm would indeed be 'The farm enclosed by the Vina': Vinagardr.**

Gardr is an enclosure but carries the intent of protection as in our guard. It can mean stronghold, castle in ON. Note also ON vard, to defend, to hold a place. Did we once have Vinavard? This site may be ancient in use. Analyses by the author of possible solstice observation sites in Wirral strongly suggest the ridgeline here was such as site, exploiting hill notches in the Clwydian Hills (31). Dibbin may be Debden = deop + denu, in Old English = deep valley, an accurate description. However we also have OE dub, dubban to strike, with Swedish dubbe and Icelandic (ON) dubba and dybba of similar meanings. Possibly we have Dubba dale or Dybba dale: the dale of strikes, blows. This name could extend the area of conflict from Vineyard Farm eastwards towards Bromborough village or north eastwards towards Spital dam across Dibbin valley.

Just north of Spital dam we note fields (nos. 149, 153, 156) called Tungrave. Tun is a settlement. Grave can be a grove but also simply a grave. ON grafa means to dig, to bury. In ON a grove is lundr. All the fields are marked as open arable land in 1839.Was there conflict along the eastern Dibbin as well as the western Clatterbrook? Bromborough Pool is 2/3 of a mile to the north and the Dibbin was once navigable beyond the current dam site at high tide.

Did a Norse war party come upstream from the pool and did the local Norse settlers foolishly guest them until Mercians arrived from Poulton 'Castle'? Did the Mercians then march on eastwards to Lathegestfeld and kill more Norse at Wargraves and The Hales? We should also ask if Vinheidi/Vinheidr is the same battle as Brunanburh. Well Brunanburh is also named as Wendune in some sources. Was this also, simply, Venduna or Vinduna? Recall that V in ON is pronounced W. Verbal transmission of the story would change V to W. Dune is just another word for heath but in ON duna means a thunderous noise. Did we have Wenduna, Vinaduna, the Vina river of thunder?

In English we still have 'din: a tumult, clash, uproar, *clatter...*'
We have recovered the same meaning as in Clatterbrook. That seems
a curious coincidence. But also a dun in the Celtic languages is a fort
giving again, Wendun, the Fort on the Vina, perhaps at Poulton Hall
just south of the farm itself. Related to this name we have the battle
of Duinbrunde recorded during the time of Constantine II, in The
Chronicles of the Kings of Alba. Brunde seems to be our Bruna and
duin can be a fort or rath; specifically, usually a circular earthen
enclosure with ditches hosting a flat topped, raised mound. This
could be applied to Brimstage or Poulton Hall.

However, since Egil was a skald, some interpreters apply poetical or
allegorical meanings to these various names. So vinheidi has been
read as vinheidr were the adjective 'heidr' means bright and the
noun 'heidr' means honour. Vine honour or vine bright, make no
sense but if 'Vina' is a local river name they do: Vina of honour
...river of honour and bright Vina... bright river. In Scandinavian
mythology of course the Vina (or Dwina) was one of nine rivers
flowing from Midgard to Niflheim, the world of darkness and cold,
 poetically appropriate for a river traversing a site of mass death
perhaps.

Vin or vinr is also a patron or leader. So we could have 'the leader's
heath' and so on. However just to turn the screw, Vina, a proper
noun, has also been read as vinna to win and vinur or victory.
This gives us several interesting combinations:

Vinheidi = vinurheidi = victory heath
Vinheidr = vinurheidr = victory of honour
Vinuskogar = vinurskogar = victory woods
Vinaheidr = Vina, river of honour
Vinaskogar = Vina river woods.

For completeness I note ON 'eyda' meaning to destroy, to lay waste,
giving Vineyda, Vina, river of destruction.These names seem
appropriate as epithets for the great Battle of Brunanburh where
according to the Anglo-Saxon Chronicle, 'five kings and seven earls'
and 'countless of their host' were slain and the long term fate of
England and Britain was decided: the Mercia –Wessex alliance beat

the Norse-Irish-Scots-Welsh axis (and some sources claim 35,000 casualties). Since Egil and his brother fought with their own war band on the side of King Aethelstan and Egil was a skald (poet) on the make, his possibly fulsome description of the battle area (and his own role) is understandable. However perhaps the locals, who were a mix of Romano-British Celts and Norse with a thin veneer of Anglo-Saxon, wishing to appear loyal to Mercia, applied similar fulsome terms to local places after the battle.

Was Vineyard Farm a memory of 'Vinagardr', the enclosure or Castle on the Vina, or 'Vinurgardr', the 'Victory enclosure'? Interesting curved soil marks are still present in the unusual, elliptical northern field of Vineyard Farm. The remains of a fortified enclosure, perhaps? But was Vinheidi even a real place? Well one key verse in one version of Egil's Saga suggests so:

> 'Flame-hearted Thorolf, fears foe, Earl-killer
> Who so dared danger in Odin's dark wars, is dead at last.
> Here *by Vina's green bank*, my brother lies under earth.'

Egil's slain berserker brother was buried on the banks of the Vina ...a real river it seems, after all. Surely even Egil the Skald would not confabulate on the circumstances of his brother's death? There is other evidence of Egil's attitude to fallen kin. Egil is known for the unconventional (in skaldic poetry), deeply personal, memorial poem in praise of his dead son Bodvar: 'Sonatorrek' (10). The boy drowned around 960 AD and Egil laments the impossibility of taking revenge on the sea gods as he would wish to do. Unusually he also blames Odin for his suffering: Odin, 'Lord of the Spear', whom he had served as a warrior all his life. I suggest that Egil spoke the truth about the burial of Thorolf on Vina's bank.

Is Thorolf still there, laid to rest with his well forged weapons as Egil tells us? Are the two golden arm bracelets still where Egil placed them on his brother's body? The large recent find of many metal artefacts at Poulton Lancelyn suggests much may yet survive across the battlefield. If this seems doubtful remember Schleimann, led by Homer's recorded place names to long fabled Troy and to Mycenae, rich in gold.

Tithe maps of Poulton Lancelyn (1839) show mainly conventional field names with a few exceptions worth noting for future research. The field name of the proposed weapons camp is 'Alleloons' (22). A loon is simply a selion or land strip of area 1 furlong x 1 chain. Alle is all in German and presumably Saxon. Aller in ON is whole, entire...a very similar meaning. But remember holl in ON means the heavenly hall as in Valholl, Valhalla, and haele also means hero. Did we have 'Haeleloons', the field of heroes? But two OI words are noted for later research: allta, wild, furious and allguth, a great noise or shouting, giving the field of fury or shouting. Curiously in ON allhardr means violent.

The position of Alleloons was close to Poulton Hall and Vineyard Farm and south east of the presumed main action. However its choice as a recovery camp may also be because it lies on the old east / west path from Bromborough Village to Heswall and the west coast. The path crosses the southern boundary of Clatterbridge Hospital and the eastern Roman road. Conflict names begin just to the north of here and stretch all the way to Prenton. The Roman road would be the best way to bring recovered weapons south to a recovery camp near the presumed burh near Poulton Hall.
To the west our path crosses the western Roman road near several conflict fields on the tentatively identified, most southerly, western escape route. Our old path could again transport recovered weapons from the western conflict sites eastwards to the Alleloons recovery site.

A day or so before the main battle recall that the Norse sent a probing force to the Mercian tent camp (also at Poulton Lancelyn?) and were repulsed and slaughtered...according to Egil's Saga.
We should also remember that Vineyard Farm was long part of the Poulton Lancelyn estate with the Hall just ¼ mile to the south. Poulton Hall stands on high ground with much lower ground to the west, south and east, above the deep Clatter / Dibbin valley. The plateau is also large enough for a burh. Old maps showed a castle at the site as mentioned earlier. However no convincing stone work has ever been found but this does not preclude wooden stockades and earth works there in Saxon times. Of course this site is also enclosed by our proposed Vina River. Perhaps the fortified Hall site itself was known as Vina Gardr, the Vina Castle?

Brunanburh may mean the stronghold of Bruna and this could have been at the Poulton Hall site although the stronghold is often simply assumed to be at the old moated Court site near Bromborough Pool. Nevertheless the author favours his conclusion that the western ancient strong point of the Brunanburh area was the 'Cliff Fort' at Brimstage while accepting that many of the water related names we found at Brimstage could also be applied to the Poulton site. Either way the existence of a possible 'Vina River' castle or burh at Vineyard Farm or Poulton Hall adds considerably to the evidence that the great battle of Brunanburh took place in this area of Wirral.

Just north of Poulton Hall on Vineyard Farm is a pair fields (nos. 108 and 113) with a strange name worth recording: 'Yolk of Egg' (22). To the author this immediately suggested an earlier name rendered into a memorable, spoken English equivalent. The author then recalled that egg in ON means egg but *also* 'edge'. In ON this has interesting consequences. 'Eggprima' means a clash of edges, a kenning for battle. 'Eggtog' means drawing of the edges, of the swords and likewise, a battle.

Is 'yolk of egg' a distorted kenning for a battle? Two other ON words for battle are jara (pronounced yara) and hlokk. Did a skaldic repetition of battle terms, using yara lokk become yolk? This kind of complex kenning is well known in Norse epic poetry.

Very strangely, as we will see again below, 'of' may be 'odr' which means raging, berserk...did Egil name these fields? We also note the still current Norse personal name 'Jokell' which is a merger of the ON names Jo and Ketill. Was Yokell of Edges, Yokell the Swordsman, one of Egil's fallen mercenary warriors buried here? As usual there is a good alternative.

A yoke is an old unit of land measurement. It was the area that could be ploughed by a yoke (pair) of oxen in a day. It is related to the Roman jugerum and the Germanic languages, joch. So we would have fields called 'yoke of edges' that is simply, field of edges, field of swords. Is this a battle memory or were battle swords found there by later residents as happened further north? However yoke is usually found in the south of England.

Curiously on Wirral a further we noted that four adjacent tithe fields share the name 'yolk of egg' in Tranmere (Derby Road) west of the ancient Tranmere inlet and beech, one possible site for a Norse fleet landing. This is north east of Storeton and on one obvious escape route from the battlefield to the eastern end of Wallasey Pool. *All the accessible 'yolk of egg' fields are worth careful archaeological examination.*

Our interest in this area should be further enhanced by the fields called Lamperloons and Top Lamperloons on Lancelyn Farm just west of Poulton Hall. To lamp someone still means to strike them. However the term appears to be very old. Cassell's Dictionary of Slang tells us:

'Lamp verb: early 19th century and still in use : to beat or strike or thrash.
Lam verb: 16th century and still in use : to beat or strike; thus lamming, a beating, linked to Old Norse lemja, to lame as a result of a beating.'

The Oxford Dictionary gives us

'Lamp verb, dialect (chiefly northern) and slang [of uncertain origin; possible alteration of the verb lam. Cf. Old Norse lemja (past tense lamoa), literally 'to lame' (= Old English lemian, from lama lame,) but chiefly used with reference to beating.]

We have the field of the lampers, the beaters or lamers. These fields are some hundreds of yards south of the confirmed Mercian weapons recovery camp. Did Anlaf's probing forces at one stage get as far south as the Poulton Hall / Vineyard strongpoint? Or were Norse prisoners (and local Norse farmer collaborators) taken to the Vineyard site for interrogation and punishment after the battle? In relation to this the tithe field next to Lamperloons is called the 'Chaltral Field'. Chal is old dialect for a person. More interestingly chaltral in Welsh means calculus, originally from the Latin for small pebble. Such pebbles or calculi, where used to record counts of farm livestock. So perhaps the owners of the 'Vina Castle' kept and counted sheep here. Or was this field where the battle prisoners were kept and counted? Interesting coincidences perhaps.

The name Poulton Lancelyn also deserves more consideration given the above names. The family first appears in the record via the name Scirard de Lancelyn. Now sometimes landowner families take the name of the place they hold rather than the reverse. Either way the name is interesting. Lancelyn is sometimes read as a version of the Old English, Lancelot and this has ignited romantic and imaginative Arthurian links, and Sir Gawain and The Green Knight certainly includes references to 'the Wilderness of Wirral' where 'few lived who loved with a good heart, either God or man'. We could at a stretch, read Lance Lynn which becomes the Lake of Lance(lot) or the Stream of Lance(lot)! More literally, we have simply the River of Lances (...a place where a host of Saxon cavalry camped?). Was the, probably, local author of the Green Knight inspired by the traditional Lancelot connection with Poulton Lancelyn? Perhaps this *was* Sir John Stanley of Storeton Hall who also wrote his home into the story as the Green Chapel.

Lancelyn could also be read as Llan Celyn which would imply a church, or *church enclosure* by a holly wood (The Green Chapel?) An early lost chapel is recorded at Poulton Lancelyn.

An early Celtic / Roman church is not unlikely since the area was primarily Romano / British (Cornovii). In the north the Celtic Britons were still prominent in isolated Wallasey, 'The Island of the Welshmen', when the Saxons and Norsemen came. The church of St. Hilary there is, most unusually, named for a 4th century 'French' (Celtic) saint. Irby is also accepted as Ira-byr, the settlement of the Irish.

Circular church enclosures at Overchurch, Moreton, Woodchurch, Wallasey and *Bromborough* are said to strongly suggest the presence of early Celtic churches. Remember llan can also mean a church enclosure. Close by in Dibbinsdale we have St. Patrick's Well, with St. Chad's Well just east of Bromborough village and to the north west, the village of Landican or Llan Tegan and Lanacre (Upton), possibly llan acre or church acre (a priest's holding). Liscard, Irby and Noctorum are also firmly identified as Old Irish names or references. We could also read the name Lancelyn as another Celtic name: Linn Celyn or Llyn Celyn which become Holly Lake or Holly Stream: the water theme yet again which we noted in Othlynn.

The place name Poulton Lancelyn may twice record that water theme in various languages. A third of a mile south west of Poulton Hall we noted Raby Mere and nearby. This name too is of interest. The village of Raby is one and a half miles west; something which still causes regular confusion to visitors seeking the mere itself or the Wheatsheafe Inn in Raby village. Raby is often interpreted as the boundary settlement: ra – byr. However ra or vra specifically means corner in ON, not usually boundary, so we have the corner settlement. On Wirral we also have the Wro at Caldy. Vra would be pronounced Wra in speech. So what is a boundary in ON? Well mark, sign and boundary is merki. This is close to the OE word for boundary: gemaere and later, mere. This is a peculiar coincidence.

We have Raby Mere or corner settlement boundary. Was the mere, lake, here in Saxon times? It exists today because of a dam built to power a water mill. Perhaps it was once just a boundary stream. If so perhaps we should also look again at Raby. In ON we also have the word hrae which means a corpse killed in battle. Did we once have 'the place of the dead on the boundary stream'? Were significant Saxon battle dead buried here? There is more. We have argued that the main battle area was north of the Brimstage – Poulton Hall line. We also suggested that Anlaf came south along the old Roman road line while Aethelstan came north from Deva along the same road line. If his army was truly of 20,000 men it is possible that their movements were noted further south. The Roman road line is still allegedly visible along Street Hey in Willaston. To the north, on the same line, is the straight Hargrave Lane in the area of the same name. The northern end is near Raby Hall Farm, ½ mile south west of Poulton Hall.

The northern portion of the eastern Roman road in the Birkenhead area was known as Blakestrete at one time. We note that near Raby Hall is Bleakley Farm adjacent to the road line, another road memory perhaps. It is commonly said that Blaec relates to the dark ashes or cinders forming the top layer of some lesser Roman roads.

Harding and others have considered Hargrave in relation to the supposed Norse / Saxon boundary line near Raby (4). Grave is read as greave or grove. Har is read as hoary, old, venerable in OE. We have 'hoary woods'.

Harr is grey haired in ON. On this basis, since he places the Norse boundary nearby, Harding assumes har must relate to this. To be fair ancient standing stones were once called 'hoar stones'. Indeed the author believes several stones at Willaston may be Bronze Age or older but knows of none in Hargrave.

However in Appendix 2 we show that a density analysis of Norse names down the length of the Wirral suggests a very weak or non-existent boundary in the era of Brunanburh with strong population mixing. The name Hargrave first appears much later. Har may still be read as old but suppose we take grave at face value? Har like haugr in ON can also mean grave. Also in ON grafa means to dig, to bury. Haer is also an army. Herr is a warrior, host or army. We could read simply the Old Grave or the Army Grave, or if we must, 'the wood where the army camped'.

But were some of the important Saxon dead also buried here after the battle? Or did a part of Aethelstan's huge army camp here, along the Roman road and at nearby Raby Mere (for the water) and at Poulton Lancelyn after the battle?

One last curious link between Hargrave and our new interpretations of Raby Mere: OE harre means hinge as opposed to ON vra or ra, corner. *This possibility of battle related activity in the south is worth exploring archaeologically if serious consideration is given once more to the LP* **Option 2B, eastern 'Urban extension'.**
Harding also notes in discussing the Heswall area places called Harrowe Hay and Harrowby which combine our component terms. He reads owe as haugr, burial mound and harr as haerri, high. He also notes OE hearg meaning heathen shrine. We could equally say Harrhaugr, ancient grave or ancient shrine. There is, south of Raby village, the Raby Mound of uncertain date associated with local standing stones.

3.4   East of the Main Battle Site

Harding and Dodgson have also highlighted a suggestive place name just to the north east of the current Bromborough village and about 400 yards from the Mersey banks: Lathegestfeld (1412). Dodgson read this as ON leidr, or OE lad which mean unwelcome (or hateful).

Ladgest in OE would be the unwelcome guest or visitor. But leidr can also mean hateful! So we would have 'the field of the unwelcome or hateful visitor'. Harding comments with no obvious irony, 'these interpretations may refer to some local conflict in the area'.

Leida also means guide. But lata in ON means deceased and strangely, permit, concede. Lida also means, dead, to pass away, the passage of time. This would give the dead guests field. Is this Saxon irony? However in old Cheshire dialect, lathe is to ask or invite (12) so we would have the invited guest field! (cf. lata, to permit).
Perhaps the name stuck because it suited both the local 'Saxons' and the local Norse: one group resisting Anlaf's ships at Bromborough Pool and welcoming in Aethelstan's troops; one group welcoming the invaders, in memory, via the ambiguity of OE! There is another possible, related link. Large scale military organisation in Scandinavia was based on the leidang (ON leidangr, OD lethang). It is said to derive from leid meaning expedition, a following of men and gangr, going, or gagn meaning equipment, supplies. The leidangr was a levy of ships, men, armaments and supplies called together by the king (10). This appears to be a perfect description for some of Anlaf's and Constantine's fleet landing at Bromborough Pool. However there is a further military link. The Norwegian kings had two classes of retainers: hirdmenn 'the household men' and the lower order, gestir (on half pay).
The gestir acted as armed odd job men (or policemen, or mercenaries) but also collected money due to the king. It was said in the 13th century that they were widely unpopular and hence became 'unwelcome guests' in many homes, so we return to the term 'ladgest' in OE.

Perhaps these *were* Anlaf's men come ashore for conquest, looting food and supplies and finding instead, death. The area containing the old moat earthworks by the Pool is plot no. 3, Round Orchard. However it is not circular in shape. In ON rond is a shield. We should also finally note again the word lath in OI. It means rut, as in the rut of an animal. However in literary use it is a known kenning for a warrior. So we have the 'field of the warrior guests'...a leidangr camp manned by the kings (lower order) men?

A tithe map of 1731, also reproduced by Harding, shows three farm fields *at the same location as Lathegestfeld,* called 'wargraves'. This author notes that several early 6 inch and 25 inch OS maps also officially record the 'wargraves' area and assign the spot to the battle of Brunanburh in 937 AD! This name appears on the *later* tithe map of 1839 but now as 'wergreaves'. Wer of course is OE for man but also wehr is a force as in wehrmacht. Greaves are a form of leg armour with a pedigree going back to the Greek hoplite. In OE they were called ban–rift, bone defenders. While greave *could just* mean grove the *oldest map* of 1731 clearly says 'wargraves'. In ON a grove is lundr and grafa means to dig, to bury. Perhaps we *should* read lata or lida as dead. Adjacent to the 'wargraves' are four tithe fields called The Hales or sometimes Heels (22) (nos. 87, 88, 89, 100). In ON, heel is haell but we also have Hel, the goddess of the underworld, of death, in Niflheim and hael therefore is a well known kenning for death. We also note heill which means in ON, 'to bid godspeed, until we meet again' (cognate with OE hail). However there is also the word haele or hero to be considered.

We also find a nearby tithe field called Lamper Loons, from the OE, to lamp to lame, identical to the fields at Poulton. ~100 metres to the north of Wargraves, on the Mersey banks lays 'The Rice'. There was a good sized beach here stretching northwards to Bromborough Pool. Consulting various 10th century local language dictionaries is enlightening. Rice is Welsh but equivalent to Rhys and Rees which mean passionate so we have 'The Passion'. However the related 'English' words have similar meanings. ME rei, ree, reoh, is from the OE hreoh, meaning fierce, angry, wild and the Old Saxon origin is hre, evil, angry. The English dialect adjective, ree, means fierce, frenzied. More directly, in ON we note hraezla, pronounced hrizla', with a hard 'i', meaning terror, fear. Could the name recall a violent skirmish here as the Norsemen retreated to the local beach or northwards to Bromborough Pool? For completeness we also have ON rea, to vex and reisa, meaning to raise up.

The close combination of Wargraves, hero, frenzied, terror death fields is hardly a coincidence. This site is ~2.5 miles due east of the presumed centre of the battlefield. The site is a half mile or so south of Bromborough Pool, a proposed Norse – Irish fleet landing place.

Was this perhaps a significant skirmish site or did the main battle spread even further than we proposed earlier? It may be that the Norse fared badly here. Professor Harding notes an old local tradition that after Brunanburh the local Norse population favoured the Deeside landing places over the Mersey shore which was now considered to be cursed (19).

East of the battle 'centre', at St. Andrew's (Saxon, Celtic?) church, when a heating system was installed, in 1871, a mass grave of 'bones with arrow heads' was found in vaults deep beneath the church floor. The excellent church history by Richard Lancelyn Green (20) quotes 'The Hundred of Wirral' of 1889

'Under the flooring was found a large quantity of bones and skulls, many bearing evidence of wounds and violence, some even with fragments of iron and arrowheads imbedded, and numbers of arrow heads also. This would certainly point to a battle having been fought in the neighbourhood, and might be regarded as additional evidence of the great fight of Brunanburh.'

The author (as he prepared for his wedding there) was briefed on this mass grave nearly fifty years ago by the vicar, who certainly accepted the evidence. This place has been said to mark the grave of the more important Saxon battle dead. These bones unfortunately have not so far been dated despite long standing Wirral Archaeology efforts with Anglican Church authorities to gain access for that purpose. These bones are another key smoking gun. We should also look again at the old name of St. Andrews. Christianity was reintroduced into England by St. Chad in 670 AD. Lancelyn Green believes the oldest Saxon church at the Bebington site would have been of wood (or wattle and daub; 20). Sometime before the Norman Conquest it was replaced by a stone church, of which some stone rows survive: the White Church. This name was apparently sometimes applied to a stone church which replaced a previous wooden structure. However the stone from the Roman quarries at Storeton is of a white – grey colour as is the current church. There is a third, complementary explanation. We noted that vaettfang is a battle field and vaettr a spirit. V in ON is pronounced w and ae is pronounced as a hard i. So vaett could be pronounced white by Norse locals.

Did the Saxon church become known as the White Church because of the Saxon battle dead buried beneath it after Brunanburh? This and the colour of the stone reinforce each other, a recipe for name endurance in local tradition. The area was nominally Saxon but with heavy Norse-Irish settlement all around after 902 AD. Bebington is usually read as Bebba's tun, Bebba being a Saxon name. However the place may be older. Roman coins were found here and the church is on a raised mound. We should note that Bebbin was an Irish and Welsh goddess of the underworld. Perhaps we do have a pre-Christian site here?

At least two other (unfortunately unpublished) mass graves are alleged to exist in the area. I suggested Ethel's Covert earlier as one possibility. Tithe field name analyses suggest several more.
For mass burials the area has many convenient marl and clay pits and meres and there is a forested Roman quarry site at Umberstone Covert at Brackenwood, south east of Storeton. Perhaps the Dead Man's Wood? According to Egil the Skald's battle description, King Aethelstan may have made his personal stand on the adjacent fields.

One, last, strange link. The sandstone at Storeton varies in colour from light grey to red. Some old stones appear to darken after long exposure. Umber is a redish-brown colour. Our old friend 'brun' is also 'brown'. Did a tall, standing stone once mark the place of the battle?

Or is the name older? Several standing stones once stood close by, at Needwood Farm and there are still old, umber coloured standing stones in the woods along Mount Road. Where these pre-Roman stones or medieval merestones? Umber is from Latin umbra, shadow, darkness. Shadow stones perhaps suggests stones associated with death, an ancient grave site? But see below. One wonders how old the name Needwood is. It is interesting to note that naud(r) in ON is harm, difficulty, distress which would be a good name for a wood through which thousands fled and died. A search found only one other Needwood in England. Needwood Forest is near Burton in Staffordshire. It is said to mean 'Forest of Refuge' in Middle English. Very curiously this wood has been associated since the 15th century in local legend with the Green Knight just as nearby Storeton is on Wirral.

Needwood Farm & Brimstage Road

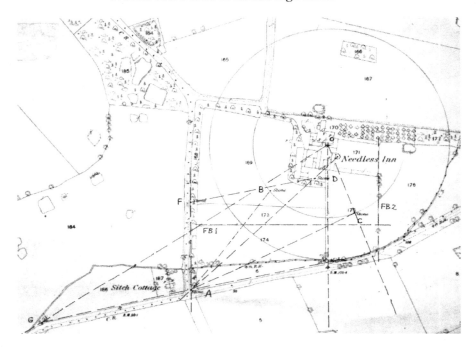

Needwood Farm drew the author's attention some years ago for another reason. Mid 19th century 6 inch and 25 inch OS maps show standing stones marked on the Farm fields not associated with contemporary boundaries (see Appendix 3). The figure above shows the stones on a 25 inch OS map. To the east of the farm buildings is a dotted circle with a central dot. In other contexts this denotes a stone circle or a cairn circle. The Ordnance Surveyors were usually careful to discriminate between boundary stones, gate posts and stones they believed to be ancient.

One battered stone still stands alone on the Brakenwood Golf Course and one at the waste recycle centre, at or near their original positions. Apart from other sandstone fragments beneath the trees and one partly buried, but large stone, all else is gone. Needwood is now part of a WMBC municipal golf course and unfortunately it has proved impossible to identify the old tithe field names on the site.

One wonders if the 'cairn circle' and the stones memorialised the centre of the Brunanburh battle field but the stones may be much older. Recent analysis shows that the Needwood stones and others by Clatterbridge Hospital are related and form a geometrical array with many alignments to calendrical and astronomical horizon events in the Neolithic & Bronze Age. Across Mount Road from Needwood we noted Umberstones Covert earlier but to the west of the covert are several large fields called simply Umberstones , adjacent to the Roman road and clearly on the battlefield. One wonders if other ancient standing stones, related to the Needwood stones once also stood there. One remained on early OS maps. We noted that umber means shadow, darkness. Is umber then a memory of the calendrical use of the local stones: an observational / ritual site used during darkness?

The Saxon country folk are known to have venerated and even worshipped ancient standing stones despite Christianisation.
The Needwood site would have been a well known landmark. Some historians have suggested that great battles like Brunanburh took place at an agreed time and location. Egil's Saga claims this for our battle. Aethelstan was the grandson of Alfred The Great who had a famous victory against the Danes at Edington in May 878 A.D. The chronicles tell us that Alfred rallied the men of Wiltshire, Somerset and Hampshire to his cause at Egbert's Stone, site uncertain.
One candidate is a boundary stone where Somerset, Wiltshire and Dorset meet. Was this an ancient co-opted standing stone? (In Liverpool we can point to the Neolithic Calderstones tomb, the Rodger Stone and Pyke Lowe which, still in recent centuries, marked administrative and land ownership boundaries). A more interesting Egbert site was Court Hill at Kingston Deverill, south of Warminster, where four standing stones, possibly the remains of a Neolithic chambered tomb or a dolmen, once stood and also known as Egbert's Stones. The stones were moved to the village church and still exist there. The use of ancient stones as rallying points in Saxon England seems to be confirmed.

 So did the ancient 'sacred' stones at Needwood set the location of our battle? We should also note that the Saxons sometimes buried their dead by ancient mounds and stones. Did this happen at Needwood?

It is curious that Aethelstan means 'Noble Stone'. Needwood Farm / Clatterbridge is one of ~20 identified standing stone sites on Wirral with special calendrical properties (18, 30,31). We already noted the stones at Irby. In total ~180 old standing stones have been identified to date across Wirral on old OS maps.

So far we have looked at the area east of the main battlefield assuming men fleeing eastwards from the central Clatterbridge / Brakenwood battle area. We noted the two Tungrave fields on the same route at Spital. However tithe field analysis showed that the battle front moved northwards through Storeton and Little Storeton with troops fleeing northwards towards Wallasy Pool and westwards towards Thingwall, the western Roman road, Meols and the Dee coast. Troops fleeing eastwards from Little Storeton through Storeton Woods for Bromborough Pool, the Mersey tidal inlets and to the wide beach north of the Pool (which extended to Tranmere Inlet), would pass through Higher Bebington and Port Sunlight. Here we find other interesting tithe field names.

Going eastwards we first find Jackson's Greaves on Higher Bebington recreation ground with Little Short Butts and Big Short Butts to its south. There is no indication of groves or woods on the early maps. Do we have graves? In ME butts were originally targets for archers. The adjacent Bebington High School now occupies 'Threat Meadow'. To the east we find several large fields called 'Stones' near Bebington Station. Part of this area near the Oval is still open. There is no sign of loose stones on the surface. The only other stone field known to the author was on Mount Road by one of the old Storeton quarries where large stones were cut.

The author, for the record, wonders if the Stones fields once hosted another standing stones site. This area is intriguing. East of the Stones several large fields straddle the railway line, called Hogshead and Big Hogshead. We noted earlier that hogg means blow, execution, behead in ON. Hogg-orrosta means close, hand to hand, fighting. However hogshead may be derived from the Scandinavian languages in a second way. Hogshead was originally oxhuvud in OS and oxehoved in OD. In ON head is hofod but ox means axe. We could read the field names as 'axehead'. We have two conflict related possibilities in agreement, a recipe for name preservation.

Straddling the railway line just south of Bebington Station we have two plots called 'Wall Field'. In ON valr is corpse slain in battle, pronounced walr. These plots are adjacent to the Dibbin / Mersey inlet near the upper point of normal high tides, linking directly to Bromborough Pool. The Pool and the inlets could hold dozens of long ships or supply ships and the adjacent long beach, from The Rice northwards, many more. At the Pool in the location of the old 'moat' earthworks we have the 'Round Orchard'. But this field is irregular and not round. We note again that in ON, rond is one name for a circular shield.

3.5 A Final Suggestion

Here is one suggestion for further study. Many have pointed to the huge number of rake names in Wirral. Rak is just lane in ON. Harding counted 96. However we also have rekkr in ON, meaning warrior. This author counts 18 ON names between 'Wargraves' and Poulton Hall in a nominally 'Saxon' area, including 6 rakes. There are another 6 rake names in the Brimstage / Storeton area. We are in Brunanburh battle territory here. Perhaps some of these were once 'rekkr', warrior, names. We have for example Rake Hey Covert, or possibly, Rekkr Hey, the Warrior's Field, 600 yards south of Storeton Hall by Rake Low.
Low is said to be from OE hlaw, a hill, a burial mound. We also have hoh and haugh and ON haugr, with the same meaning. But note also ON hrekja, to drive away, rout. On Wirral Stanlow, Stanhlaw, is well accepted, as is Hooton or Haughtun. So at Storeton do we have Rekkrhlaw, the Warriors' Grave perhaps? Well the Rake Hey Covert land was previously ploughed as the ridge and furrow lines attest, perhaps in Medieval times, but on the Lidar scan a faint ellipse can be seen in its centre which is about 70 ft across on the long axis.

Is this a ploughed out tumulus or a bank / ditch mass grave marker? Is this covert The Deadmen's Wood? Remembering Egil's description of the routed Norsemen I also note ON reka, to avenge, to pursue a fleeing force. In English we still wreak revenge and havoc. Also in English, reek means to smell badly! Despite the proposed name the site could be of any date back to the Bronze Age.

However the presence of The Arno in Birkenhead, Arnis-haugr or Arneshow, the presumed burial mound of the local Norse landowner, Arni, tells us the ellipse could also be the remains of a 10th century burial place.

Rake Hey Covert at Storeton

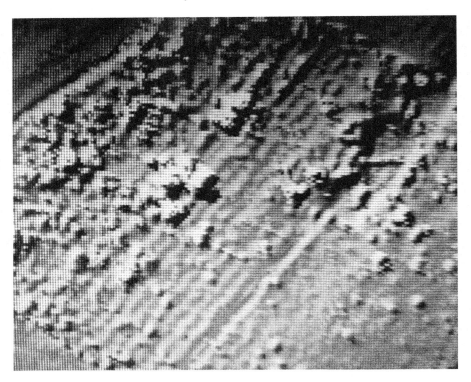

Section 3.6   The Dingesmere Problem

> 'The Norsemen left them in their well-nailed ships,
> The sad survivors of the darts, on Dingesmere
> Over the deep sea back they went to Dublin,
> To Ireland they returned with shameful hearts.'

The Anglo-Saxon Chronicle

The location of Dingesmere is unresolved to the point where some analysts declare it to be mythical ...a mere literary or poetic device, not now understood.

The same idea you will recall was applied wrongly, to Vinheidi. Harding has proposed that Dingesmere was the name of the stretch of the Dee near Dawpool and Red Bank on the west coast of Wirral.

His reasoning is that Thingwall and the site of the Norse Thing was just three miles inland and that the long beach served the Thing as a local harbour. This is not unreasonable. However what applies to the Dee also applies to the south Lancashire coast and the Mersey.
 From Birkdale southwards and within a few miles of the coast, there are nineteen certain, major Norse place names. There are a further eighteen Norse place names inland of the coastal zone and several more in east Lancashire. There are many minor place names. This activity explains why a second Thing existed near Thingwall Hall in the Knotty Ash / Board Green area of Liverpool. There was an apparent earthwork south east of the hall. This is about three miles inland from the coast. Did the Liverpool Thing area also have a port? Well, there was an inlet and tidal pool on the Mersey at the original site of Liverpool town which became the first dock site. There is one other name in England which is suggestive: Mersea Island in Essex. This is said to derive from OE 'meresig' meaning 'island of the pool'. It appeared in the Domesday Book as Meresai. But there is a better candidate.

Opposite Bromborough Pool, one of the possible landing sites for Anlaf's ships, south of Dingle Point on the old OS maps, is the long Jericho Beach. Many ships could rest there. In the north the beach ends in two sandy inlets, ringed by low cliffs, which each could hold several more ships. The larger was called Knott's Hole. By coincidence Nott of course is the Norse Goddess of night and mother of Dag.

Knott's Hole leads into Dingle Glen, which runs northwards inland.
 A quarter of a mile along the glen on the east side was a high bank / earthwork on which stood the large house, West Dingle. Was this site once a burh defending the way to the South Lancashire Thing? West of Nott's Hole is more high ground edged by cliffs on the river, another good defensive position. The Dingle certainly appears to have been a significant landing place given the area just inland: Toxteth.

At Brimstage (Brunstath) and Bromborough we had Brunanstaepa as one incarnation of the name in which staepa is ON, a river landing place.

Knott's Hole in the 18th Century

So we could have Toki's river landing place. (Further inland near Thingwall, on a stream, we have Croxteth: Croki's river bank).
I suggest trade between the two Thing areas passed directly across the Mersey at slack tide, between Knott's Hole and Bromborough Pool. The alternative was the long land route upstream and across not always friendly Saxon territory.

In Scotland there was once a Dingwall associated with a local Thing as at Thingwall, Liverpool. Did we have originally the Thing / Ding Glen, the valley leading to the Thing, which later became The Dingle? However Dingle has also been interpreted as Dingyll or Den Gyll, valley ravine. Denu in Old English is valley and gyll is a gil or ravine in ON. However 19th century photographs show a wide valley beyond Knott's Hole with sloping sides, not a ravine. Around Britain we have name variants such as Dingwall, Dingel, Dingal, Dingall... which raise other possibilities. Recall that hallr in ON relates to a slope, hill, big stone, flat rock giving Dinghallr.

These names apply well to Knott's Hole beach, surrounded by sandstone cliffs and leading into the sloping valley on the way to the Thing.

Consider also one last, famous Dingle, in County Kerry, Ireland. Following vigorous debate, the town name Dingle, imposed by the British long ago as their version of the place name, is now at least complemented by the original Gaelic name: An Daingean, The Fort, in OI. Did our Dingle, whatever its origin in English place names, also once have the meaning of fort in Celtic, pre-Saxon or later Norse-Irish settlement times?

Curiously another Wirral location may support this interpretation. At Shotwick on the old Dee coastline is a large earthwork mound. At the end of the 11th century a motte and bailey 'castle' was founded there by Hugh Lupus. Adjacent to it is the once large, Dingle Wood. Did the largely Celtic (Romano – British or even Norse-Irish) locals name the wood after the castle, that is, the Wood of an Daingean, the fort? Perhaps the original site was in fact pre-Norman and pre-Saxon. The 'Norman' mound sits within a polygonal, banked enclosure. Harding insists Shotwick was a Saxon stronghold before the Normans came and built their castle (4) but the site is reminiscent of a 'Scottish' (Celtic) duin or rath of possible earlier date.

Back to the Mersey. If we do have two significant Things as political / administrative centres for the considerable Norse populations of south Lancashire and Wirral, it follows that there must have existed an *agreed* boundary between them. Well the Mersey lies between them. 'Maeres ea' in Anglo-Saxon means boundary river. Much later a 'meresman' was still the parish officer responsible for re-marking and monitoring boundaries.

Merestones, even on early 19th century OS maps, were also marked as boundary stones. It has been shown that the Mersey was long part of the major political boundary between Mercia and 'Northumbria' and 'Strathclyde' at various times. Surely the same was true at the time of the local Norse communities?

In which case did we have the 'Boundary between the Things'

for the local river name, something like 'Ding Maeres ea' and through careless transliteration by the (distant), Saxon creator of the epic Brunanburh poem in the Anglo-Saxon Chronicle, 'Dingesmaere'.

Dingle Glen in the 19th Century

There may be one last clue in the epic Anglo Saxon Chronicle poem:

'There the Norsemen's chief was put to flight
And driven by dire need, with a small retinue, to seek his ship
The ship pressed out to sea, the King departed onto the yellow flood...'

Anlaf escapes by ship. He departs on 'the yellow flood'. That is, an ebbing flood tide in some major river heavily loaded with silt. The Mersey is not yellow. However 'yellow' is not an accurate translation. The original line is 'on fealone flod'. According to the Bosworth – Toller Anglo Saxon Dictionary, fealone means 'a yellow or red tone as of withered leaves, or dusky brown'. Any local can attest to the light brown silt load carried downstream on each ebbing tide. The Mersey even at its best and in sunlight is never a blue river. The Mersey has a 30ft tidal range and powerful rip currents.

Any Wirral or Liverpool local who has stood on the Mersey bank at peak flood can testify to the power of that rushing flow and shudders at the thought of falling into it. One of the fastest flow sections, as the river narrows, is between the Devil's Bank and Jericho Beach, just south east of Knott's Hole. (A friend of the author remembers a family story that many years ago a corroded sword and shield boss were found on Otterspool (Jericho) beach but I can find no sign of them in records.) By comparison the eastern Dee ebb tide is a shallow trickle.

The heated debate about the location of Brunanburh also provides a last clue which could be seen as supportive of Wirral. In 1840 workmen found a very large hoard of Viking silver at Cuerdale (from cuer, Old French, heart) on the River Ribble near Preston (10). It consisted of 8,500 pieces of silver with a total weight of 88 lbs. It contained coins from Scandinavia, Europe and the Arab empire, the latest dated to 905 AD. The hoard must have been buried after this date. If coins were added until close to its burial, the Cuerdale Hoard can have nothing to do with Brunanburh as some still claim. It was very likely a 'Viking' war chest but from an earlier context. Remember that Aethelfleda repulsed the attacks of Ingimund earlier in the century and refortified Chester in 907 AD. Did some of the local chiefs flee north to Strathclyde or Northumbria with their treasure? Remember she allegedly dedicated a new monastery at Bromborough in 912 AD, suggesting the local Norse trouble makers like Ingimund had been eliminated or expelled.

It is just possible that a *full* chest was sealed after 905 AD and kept, perhaps with other active war chests by some important Norse (or Scottish) Lord. By 937 there was a considerable presence of Norsemen in Lancashire and Wirral as we have seen. When Anlaf invaded did local settlers and chiefs flock to his cause?There was a Thing in both Wirral and south Lancashire. When Anlaf was defeated at Brunanburh we know the Norse-Irish, Scots and Cumbrians scattered and fled homewards. Perhaps some Wirral and Lancashire chiefs and fighters fled with them.

The proposed fortified Dingle landing site on the Mersey bank across from Bromborough Pool would provide a quick route north by land across Lancashire, avoiding the harrying Mercian troops

on the Wirral and at Chester. Did some chiefs or even Kings
Constantine and Owain take that route with their remaining treasure
chests, to end at Cuerdale, on the Ribble, waiting for rescue ships
which never came? Did the Mercians eventually attack them there,
forcing the hiding of the hoard? We can only wonder if other hoards
are still there, buried along the banks of the Ribble...or west of
Brunanburh. On the other hand some claim Anlaf, Constantine
and Owain all left by sea.

3.7 The Main Brunanburh Battle Area?

The distribution of the main name locations discussed in the text is
shown on the map below. The wide distribution of suggestive
'conflict' names defines a large area across central Wirral. The
author suggests that this reflects a number of features of the 'battle'
supported by the ancient written descriptions.

1. A central battle area marking the main battle between the
   Mercian and Norse-Irish armies. I suggest the centre was in the
   Clatterbridge / Brakenwood area in land along the Roman road
   eastwards to at least Mount Road while some names suggest action
   also at Clatterbridge Hospital.
2. An area between Junction 4 and Poulton Lancelyn, marking the
   Norse-Irish pre-battle incursion into the Mercian vanguard camp at
   Poulton Lancelyn and their rout and flight northwards towards
   Storeton. The post – battle weapon recovery site with its thousands
   of confirmed finds is also here. Vineyard Farm / Poulton Hall may
   have been a Mercian, eastern strongpoint with tithe field name
   evidence indicating some violent activity here.

3. Several areas probably marking running fights along Norse-Irish
   escape routes from the battlefield to the invasion fleet landing sites
   or ports.

a). The area from Junction 4 westwards through the Brimstage area to the
western Roman road and north west to Meols or through Heswall to the
west coast.

b). The area from Junction 4 northwards to Storeton, Little Storeton and then Prenton Golf Course, marking a movement of the battle centre as the Norse-Irish shield wall broke and perhaps a series of running battles as they fled. From the suggestive name location patterns there may be four paths: northwest from Little Storeton through Landican and Arrowe Park to the western Roman road and Meols; westwards from Little Storeton to Thingwall, Irby, Thurstaston and the Dee coast at Dawpool; due north across the Arno and along Blake Street Roman road to Wallasey Pool; north eastwards from Little Storeton to Tranmere beach and Pool and possibly the eastern end of Wallasey Pool.

c). Eastward escape from Storeton and Little Storeton through Higher Bebington to Mersey inlets at Port Sunlight and Bromborough Pool. The often dismissed site of 'Wargraves' south of Bromborough Pool may have been a Viking expedition camp / strongpoint and perhaps a major skirmish did take place there before or after the main battle. We also added the Hales tithe fields and The Rice sites as evidence of action here.

4. Possible battle related activity near Raby Mere in the form of more Mercian camps along the old Roman road line, as suggested by local place names and the possibly large size of Aethelstan's army.

In Conclusion

Including 'fighting retreat' areas, camps and graves the Author suggests the main 'military action' area can be largely defined by the local streams: by the north – south Prenton Brook (The Athlyn) to the west; by the west to east line from Brimstage along the Clatterbrook feeder streams to their old junction at Clatterbridge (part of the Vina river system), south eastwards to the junction with the Dibbin and then north eastwards, around Poulton Hall, to Bromborough Pool; plus possible camps to the south near Raby Mere.

To the north the extended battle action can, based on tithe field names, be traced as far as the Prenton boundary and tentatively, almost to Tranmere Beach.

To the west the conflict tithe field names take us through possible skirmish sites and Norse- Irish settlements to the Dee coast at Dawpool and along the western Roman road towards Meols.

To the east we may reasonably suspect escape action through Higher Bebington and Port Sunlight to the Mersey inlets, Bromborough Pool and the wide adjacent beaches. To the south we have the tantalizing outliers at Wargraves / Hales and The Rice on the Mersey coast by a good beach.

Overall the place name evidence from the sagas and historic sources seems to be compatible with the landscape features of the proposed Wirral battle field of Brunanburh, and with many old, conflict, warrior, weapon related and grave, tithe field names in the 10th century local languages and later local dialects, and to a surprising degree after so many centuries. Much material may yet endure across the Wirral green belt land.

This book has been about evidence for the location of the Brunanburh Battlefield and escape routes. However Wirral has long been settled.

In looking at the Brunanburh action landscape we seem to recover signs of earlier presence back to Roman times, with the role of the eastern road to Wallasey Pool, and perhaps sites dating back to the Neolithic. The several areas outlined strongly on the battle field map overleaf are *council defined* and recognized 'Areas of Archaeological Interest' such as Vineyard Farm / Poulton Hall, Storeton, Brimstage, Barnston fields, Cross Hill / Thingwall, Landican, Irby and Thurstaston.

These areas of established antiquity all play a role in the proposed main battle site of Brunanburh and in the proposed camps and escape routes, defined by old lanes and paths, Roman roads and dozens of conflict related tithe fields.

The connections seem quite clear considering the span of time involved. The battle centre is near Clatterbridge and Needwood Farm where ancient, perhaps Neolithic, stones once stood.

Was the battle site pre-chosen to take place near this, then well known, standing stone site? The Anglo-Saxons at the time certainly still respected and even worshipped at such sites and sometimes buried their dead there.

It may be no coincidence that in fleeing westwards to the Dee, when the shield wall fell, Norsemen passed by Thingwall and the Norse Wirral 'parliament' site, over an earlier pre-Norse, probably prehistoric, moot site by Harrock Wood and another standing stone site and the adjacent Heskeths tithe fields at Irby. Of course, with more uncanny 'good' sense, WMBC has proposed this area of Irby for major housing development in the Local Plan. It may be no coincidence that those fleeing north for Wallasey Pool passed through Ufaldi's Green and Birkenhead Park so crossing another ancient standing stone site (and a possible, early burial ground) and two more stone sites on the banks of Wallasey Pool.

In the north, on our battle escape routes we run out of conflict names but not ancient names in several languages. Besides Blake Street and the proposed western Roman road there are hints of other ancient pathways, Roman or otherwise, and these should not be neglected even in built up areas. There is much more to do. This land is old and well used and should be respected.

'Though much is taken, much abides; and though
We are not now that strength which in old days
Moved earth and heaven; that which we are, we are;
One equal temper of heroic hearts,
Made weak by time and fate; but strong in will
To strive, to seek, to find and not to yield.'

Tennyson

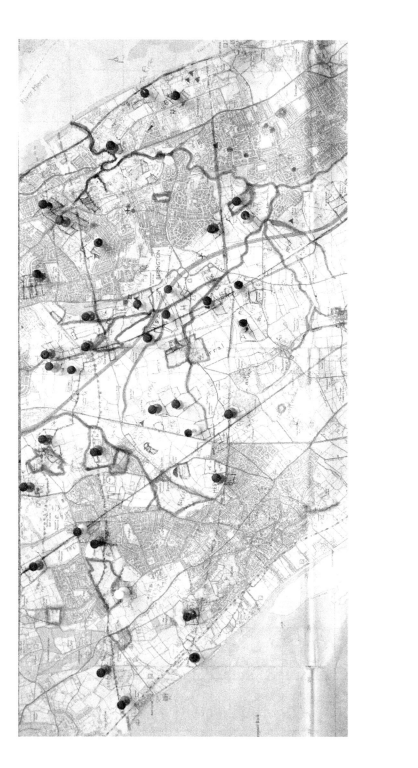

REFERENCES

1. Caville S; 'The Battle of Brunanburh in 937: Battlefield Despatches'; www.nottingham.ac.uk /-sczsteve/Cavill_2014.pdf
2. Wood M; 'Searching For Brunanburh'; Yorkshire Archaeological Journal, Vol 85, issue 1, 2013
3. Eriksson L; 'Egil's Saga' ; Penguin Classics 2004
4. Harding S; 'Ingimund's Saga : Norwegian Wirral'; Countyvise Publications, Wirral UK, 2000
5. Dodgson J; 'English Place Names : Wirral Hundred', 1972
6. Eckwall E; 'The Concise Oxford Dictionary of English Place Names', 1960
7. 'The Anglo-Saxon Chronicle'; www. britannia.com/history/docs
8. Wirral Archaeology, personal communications.
9. Tudsbury, F. W. T; 'Brunanburh A.D. 937'; Oxford University Press, 1907.
10. Foote P G & Wilson D M ; 'The Viking Achievement'; chapter 7, Sidgwick & Jackson Ltd, 1970.
11. Irvine W F; 'Wirral Place Names'; Trans. Hist. Soc. of Lancs. & Cheshire; 1891-1892, p288 on.
12. Egerton Leigh; 'Dialect of Cheshire'; 1877.
13. 'Who Wrote the Poem?'; Stephen Harding interview, Wirral News Group, 03.01.2007.
14. Morgan V and Morgan P; 'Prehistoric Cheshire'; Landmark Publishing Ltd; 2004.
15. Moffar A; 'The Faded Map: The Lost Kingdoms of Scotland'; Birlinn, 2011.
16. Chitty G; 'Wirral Rural Fringes Survey'; Journ. Of Merseyside Archaeological Society, vol 2, 1978
17. 'Making Our Heritage Matter', WBC, Wirral Heritage Strategy, 2013
18. 'Wirral & Liverpool Neolithic Solstice Sites' ; D P Gregg; 2018; report to Wirral Archaeology
19. Harding S; 'Viking Wirral'.
20. Lancelyn Green R; 'St. Andrews Bebington'; Countyvise Books, Wirral, 1993

21. Schofield G; 'The Third Battle of 1066'; History Today, October 1996
22. Cheshire Tithe Maps Online
23. Bosworth – Toller Anglo Saxon Dictionary online
24. English – Old Norse Dictionary; York University online
25. English to Old Norse Dictionary, Vikings of Bjornstad online
26. E.V. Gordon; 'An Introduction to Old Norse'; Oxford University Press, July 1981
27. Old Irish online; Linguistics Research Centre, University of Texas
28. Old Welsh – translation English / Welsh Dictionary, Lexilogos, online
29. Philpott R; Adams M; 'Irby, Wirral Excavations on a Late Prehistoric, Romano-British and Medieval Site, 1987-1996'; National Museums Liverpool, 2010
30. Gregg D P; 'A Wirral Megalithic Mystery : Ancient Stone Circles & Sacred Sites'; Green Man Books, 2018
31. Gregg D P; 'Wirral Standing Stones'; Green Man Books, 2021; submitted to the mid 2020 local plan consultation.
32. Brown A G & Meadows I, 'Roman Vineyards in Britain: finds from ther Nene valley'; Antiquity, 74 (285) pp 491-492, September 2000.
33. Darby H C, 'Domesday England'; 1977.
34. Livingston M; 'Never Greater Slaughter'; OSPREY Publishing, May 2021. (Added 18.05 21).

Appendix 1   The Intent of the Brunanburh Report to WMBC

A1.1   Local Plan Context

The 2019 Sustainability Appraisal Scoping Report section on Heritage begins by noting key messages from the NPPF

'Heritage assets should be recognised as an *'irreplaceable resource'* that should be conserved *'in a manner appropriate to their significance'*...great weight should be given to the asset's conservation...'

The Scoping Report concludes with the following WBC objective:

'***Protect, conserve and enhance heritage assets, including their setting and significance*** and contribute to the maintenance and enhancement of historic character through design, layout and setting of new development.'

The scoping report rightly notes the 26 conservation areas, 8 scheduled monuments and 14 assets at risk on Wirral. However the majority of 'official' heritage assets are individual buildings from very recent centuries. The scoping report takes a purely bureaucratic listing approach and says nothing of Wirral's long history which goes back to the Mesolithic and Neolithic (16, 18). This approach gives a distorted view of our heritage and history and automatically precludes the possibility of new insights developing and of new discoveries being taken into account in time to prevent heritage destruction. This is not in accord with the letter and spirit of the official planning guidances (see below).

The January 2020 'draft' plan 'Options & Issues', contains an interim note on Sustainability Appraisal which adds little to the 2019 document except that it refers in very general terms to the possible heritage impacts of the development options in the new draft plan ('Issues & Options'). There is no site by site discussion of the known pattern of artefacts from several periods in the Historic Environment Record in relation to the green belt sites (in particular) threatened by housing development. It does not identify several sites of known or suspected sensitivity. In relation to land parcels 'south south west of Bebington' it does note possible **'significant negative effects'** and that

'several of the parcels of land involved in an [eastern] urban extension would involve changes to the *setting* of heritage assets'

The land is not identified. *In fact this oblique reference involves the potential destruction of important parts of a major battlefield of national significance, **Brunanburh,** and not merely 'setting changes'.*

The report also fails to mention that several sites here also appear individually in the 'Dispersed green belt release', Option 2A. Remarkably the 'analysis' is even more dismissive of the western urban extension involving sites 7.15, 7.16, 7.17, 7.18 noting only *'minor negative effects'* in relation to a Grade II church. We will show this area is on the western Norse escape route from Brunanburh via Thingwall, as evidenced by many tithe field names. On the same route, we cross the large site 7.27 (Dispersed release) at Irby with similar Norse evidence (and possible battle graves) and a wealth of other historic links from several periods back to the Iron Age and Neolithic.

For the sake of certainty this report will identify the sites still at risk in the various council development options and define the probable wider battlefield area which may be put at risk as the local plan develops. We note that sites appear to come and go from various plan versions and new sites are added over time. A careful watch must be kept on heritage implications...not something so far, *pro-actively* implemented by the council.

A1.2   National Heritage Impact of Local Plan
Green Belt Release

This report looks specifically at the heritage impact of the proposed Local Plan release of green belt land for housing development in the vicinity of the M53 in the area around Junction 4 and to the west and south of J4. (Figure A). In relation to Brunanburh the area of particular concern stretches from GB parcel SP30 (Storeton) south to SP44 (Poulton Hall). To the west of the M53 battle related activity is indicated at least as far as Brimstage and on escape routes to the Dee. Roman farms have long been suspected at Storeton and Poulton (8) and a Roman road believed to link Chester and Wallasey Pool (with a branch to the Roman quarry at Umberstones Covert) is claimed to run nearby, at Clatterbridge. Recently the probable foundations of a Roman building have been reported at Poulton Lancelyn (8).

It has been suspected for many decades that the invasion of England by King Anlaf of Dublin and his allies in 937 AD was here on Wirral and that the great Battle of Brunanburh centred on the area around Brakenwood – Clatterbridge (1, 4, 9) but covered a large area from Storeton and Higher Bebington in the north, south to Brimstage at least, and along the Clatterbrook / Dibbin Valley eastwards to Poulton Hall. Pursuit of the defeated Norse army, based on the chronicles, probably continued into Prenton and beyond and to the Dee coast. Tithe field names support this. Significant skirmishes may also have occurred south of Bromborough Pool and along the tidal, navigable Dibbin towards Poulton Hall.

New analyses of the place name evidence in the chronicles and sagas add strong evidence for the battle along with many conflict related field names in the area and now major field finds at Poulton Lancelyn, outlined briefly in this report, confirm it.

A very large scatter of Viking age weapons has been found on green belt parcel **SP042** and these likely define a post battle weapons collection site (a 'bera til stangar' site) and a recovery camp of the triumphant Mercian King, Aethelstan, after the battle. It may also be the camp of the Mercian vanguard army before the battle, which is described in Egil's Saga.

Brunanburh was a huge battle, possibly involving up to 40,000 men, and marks the point in time when the realms of Mercia and Wessex became forged into one nation: England. **Brunanburh has a national significance equal to the Battle of Hastings in British history according to many historians.** The battle site of Hastings is protected and venerated. The site of Brunanburh demands equal treatment and there should be no question of further housing development there in the upcoming Local Plan. The site is an 'irreplaceable resource' in the words of the NPPF. I also note policy CH25 in 'UDP: Development Affecting Non-Scheduled Remains Policy' of the WBC.

'In assessing development proposals liable to affect areas known *or suspected to contain important un-scheduled archaeological remains*, the Local Planning Authority will in particular consider...the potential *importance of the site, in terms of rarity*, condition and estimated age of the remains...'

The national importance of Brunanburh cannot be overstated. 11.78 says

'Policy CH25 specifically provides, where the case for physical preservation in situ is overwhelming ...*for planning permission to be refused*...particularly ...*where the setting of important remains would be severely compromised.'*

Note NPPF section 16 and footnote 63

'63 Non-designated heritage assets of archaeological interest, *which are demonstrably of equivalent significance to scheduled monuments, should be considered subject to the policies for designated heritage assets.'*
Note also NPPF para 189 and 187 b) and the obligation of LAs to
'b) Predict the likelihood that *currently unidentified heritage assets*, particularly sites of historic and archaeological interest, will be discovered in the future.'
The extensive material finds on SP042 farm land suggest much material may still survive across the battlefield on the other green belt parcels described below (and to the east and west of the M53).
Historic England also stresses that

'because of their rarity, sites such as burhs, Viking camps and thegnly complexes will always be very strong candidates for listing...camps and mass graves can be included in the designated area...'

They note also that 'areas of pursuit and escape routes, after a battle line breaks', are equally important since these areas often comprise significant killing zones. The Norse were renowned for fighting retreats and local tithe field names indicate such areas here. Historic England also stresses the importance of having confirming historical documents, chronicles and epic poems: in this case we have the Anglo Saxon Chronicle, Egil's Saga and several other ancient sources. Battles with major political consequences and for 'Kingly reputations' are seen as particularly important. **All this we have here at Brunanburh**.

On the positive side, a site as important as Brunanburh offers considerable scope 'for high quality tourism' as sought by WBC policy (17) and particularly so in the year when Wirral was LCR 'Borough of Culture'. The identification of interesting conflict place names across the main battlefield and along Norse escape routes, westwards to the Dee coast, provide the basis for long distance 'battle walks', mainly in still open countryside. A modest museum convenient for the main site is also surely a reasonable investment. The value of current tourism on Wirral is over £420 million per annum.

The report will present the detailed evidence for the location of the battlefield in mid Wirral including a map of the probable area in Section 3. Figure A, below, shows the green belt parcels listed for possible release east of the M53 in the 2019 first draft local plan. The detailed report implicates all this land in the main battle, its preliminary actions and its aftermath and uses these GB parcel references as locators in discussions of the evidence. In the January 2020 draft local plan 'Issues and Options', some of these parcels have been removed but some in the centre and south remain as possible sites for development and other relevant sites have been added. (Draft LP, Map B, Map C).

Figure B shows probable retreat routes of the Norse army to local Norse settlements and invasion fleet landing places such as Wallasey Pool, Meols and Dawpool. The current draft local plan proposed sites implicated by tithe field evidence are also listed below.

Site	Comments
Sites 4.4, 4.5 Brackenwood Golf Course	close to the proposed battlefield centre
Site 4.6 just south of junction 4	" " "

FIGURE A :   Initial Green Belt Parcels Overlying the Eastern Brunanburh Battlefield

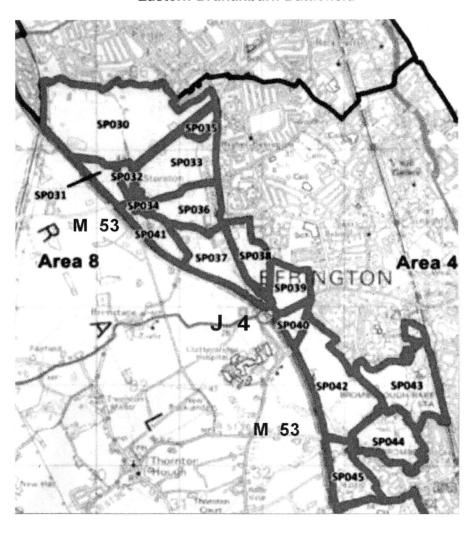

Site 4.8 Vineyard Farm ('Vina Gardr')   possible battle activity';
                                            possible site of a burh;
                                            possible Bronze Age /
                                            Neolithic site)

Site 4.10 Poulton Hall south land   possible Saxon fortification
                                            / 'castle', etc
Site 4.11 north of Raby Hall Road   (adjacent to SP042 to the

(site submitted for development by landowner)

Site 4.12 south of Raby Hall Road

Sites 7.18, 7.17, 7.16, 7.15 Option 2B

(west of Barnston Road)

Site 7.27 / SP060 (Irby / Harrock Wood area)

north; should be screened for archaeology)

(should be screened for archaeology)

(sites straddle Norse escape route to Dawpool
- Harding's proposed port of the Wirral Thing;
sites also on the Meols Roman road line)

(Norse-Irish village; site straddles escape route to Thurstaston & Dawpool port)

Figure B : Green Belt Sites on Brunanburh Escape Routes

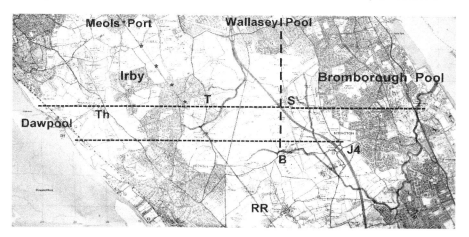

KEY

Junction 4 M53 is near the presumed battlefield centre (immediately to the west).

S is Storeton Village (Old Norse 'great settlement') and proposed Norse army camp area.

B is Brimstage (Brunanburh?).
T is the Norse Thing site near Thingwall Village.

TH is Thurstaston a Norse settlement (Thorsteinn's Tun)

RR is the conjectured western Roman road line (Defined here by a straight line from Chester North Gate to the coast at Meols along clear, linear, ancient paths in the north).

Appendix 2   The Density Distribution of Norse-Irish Place Names Across Wirral

Harding's excellent book, 'Ingimund's Saga' records in detail the location of many classes of Norse place names across Wirral and argues for a particular form for the boundary between the Norse-Irish enclave to the north and the Saxon (Romano-British) lands to the south. Considering 28 'major' place names he argues for a boundary running north eastwards from Neston on the west coast through the parish of Raby (Ra – byr, boundary settlement) to Eastham then north eastwards to Tranmere. This places Bebington, Poulton cum Spital and Bromborough to the Mersey banks, in the Saxon domain. Nevertheless this rectangular 'Saxon' wedge contains ~30 Norse place names. Similarly south of the Neston – Eastham line there are ~100 Norse names on the land. This is worth a closer look perhaps. Harding's maps use OS kilometre squares. North to south the Wirral extends from northings 690 to 940 on sheet 108 (SJ), 1: 50,000 scale OS map. If we take 1 kilometre slices west – east across the peninsula and count the number of 'Norse' place names we can calculate the average name density per kilometre square. Going north to south from the coast this gives us:

1, 1.7, **2**, 1.7, **2.8, 2.2, 4.2, 4.7, 3.3, 2.6, 3**, 1.9, 1.6, 1.3, 1.2, 1.6, 1, **2.5**, 1, 1.6, 1.1, 1, 0.3, 0.1, 0.6, 0.4

Highlighting densities above 2 shows a broad band of density in the northern third of the Wirral and a fairly constant background density to the south of this, even in the 'Saxon' zone. Density drops off between northings 820 and 830 in a strip which includes Heswall, Brimstage and Bromborough. If we look at the three north – south km slices centred on Brunanburh, the average name density in the 'Norse' zone is 1.6 and that in the 'Saxon' zone 1.5. If we look at the three north – south km slices straddling 'Saxon' Willaston (on the presumed boundary) we find a name density of 1.3 in the 'Norse' zone and 1.6 in the 'Saxon' zone.

The Norse – Irish Thing at Thingwall sits at northings 845, towards the southern end of the high Norse names density area. Was the Thing established during a period of expansion of Norse occupation southwards beyond the Neston-Raby-Eastham line?

We know that the Norse tried to push south a number of times and lusted after better farm land near Chester and indeed the treasures of Chester itself (4). By the time of Brunanburh was the Wirral population well mixed even in the south? This and the dense Lancashire and coastal Welsh settlements would surely encourage Anlaf to invade via the Wirral and make it essential for Aethelstan to oppose him there.

Was there a recognised boundary at that time? Who occupied our proposed strong points at Brimstage, Poulton Lancelyn and Bromborough Pool before the battle? Did Aethelstan first have to regain these strong points from the local Norsemen ...or during the 'Battle' of Brunanburh? The battle according to Egil occurred the morning after Aethelstan arrived in the area. Or was the Brimstage site already long abandoned?

At Bromborough in the east the action was considerably south of the Pool at the Wargraves / Hales site. All the conflict activity in the Poulton Hall area suggests the proposed Saxon 'burh' there *was* active. Aethelfleda had defeated the attack of Ingimund on Chester around 907 AD and possibly she had then expelled all the Norse trouble makers from the area. By 912 AD she is supposedly founding a monastic centre at Bromborough village which suggests more peaceful times. What happened in the following twenty five years? The sagas and chronicles unfortunately do not tell us, but by Brunanburh times there were considerable numbers of Norse traders and money lenders living peacefully in the southern end of Chester, according to Harding (19).

Appendix 3   Needwood Farm & Clatterbridge Stones
A3.1   Needwood Farm Stone Layout

Needwood Farm stood just to the north east of Junction 4 of the M53. It is now the site of Brakenwood Municipal Golf Course. On various 6 inch and 25 inch OS maps of the mid 19th century we see five standing stones with an additional stone on Brimstage Road to the west of Sitch Cottages. The Brakenwood – Clatterbridge area is probably the centre of the Battlefield of Brunanburh on which, in 937 AD, King Athelstan of England defeated a Norse –Irish – Scottish invasion army under King Anlaf of Dublin (4). Battle action appears to have engaged a large area from Vineyard Farm in the south to Storeton in the north and from Brimstage in the west to Spital in the east. Any potential 'markers' on this land are therefore of interest. However Wirral's history is long, with a Mesolithic settlement at Greasby and various Neolithic finds. The author has noted many standing stones in organized patterns which may be Late Neolithic or Early Bronze Age (5, 1). However the situation is complicated since later cultures sometimes appropriated the sites of earlier cultures as sacred sites and even burial grounds.

Figure 1   Needwood Farm & Brimstage Road

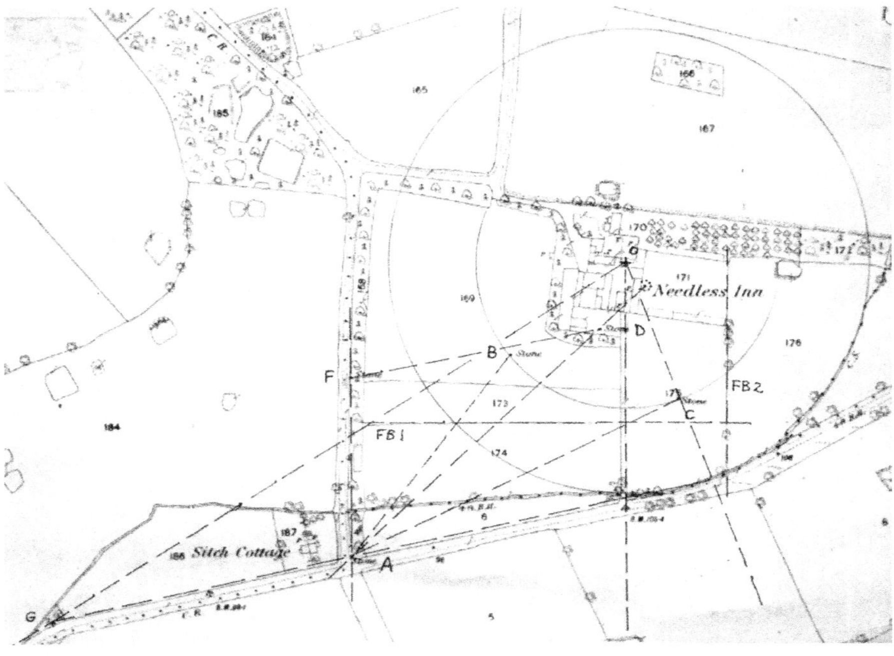

A classic case of this is the area around Stonehenge replete with wood, stone and burial mound 'markers' from the Mesolithic onwards to the Iron Age. The Saxons also reused such mounds and stones for burials but none are known on Wirral (8). It is possible that the Needwood stones were still a place of veneration by the local Saxons and indeed the Viking settlers from Ireland. In that era battles were often arraged by joint agreement on location and timing. Did our ancient stones decide the location of the Great Battle?

With the above in mind we should note in Figure 1 the small circle marked at Needless Inn. On 6 inch OS maps this looks like the symbol for a mound or small stone circle. On the 25 inch maps the shape is more defined *with a central stone* marked. This is usually the symbol for a stone cairn circle or a curb circle with a mound. It is partly overlapped by a farm building. Some agricultural purpose was first considered. A blow up and reconstruction is shown in Figure 2.

Figure 2   Possible 'Cairn Circle' Reconstruction

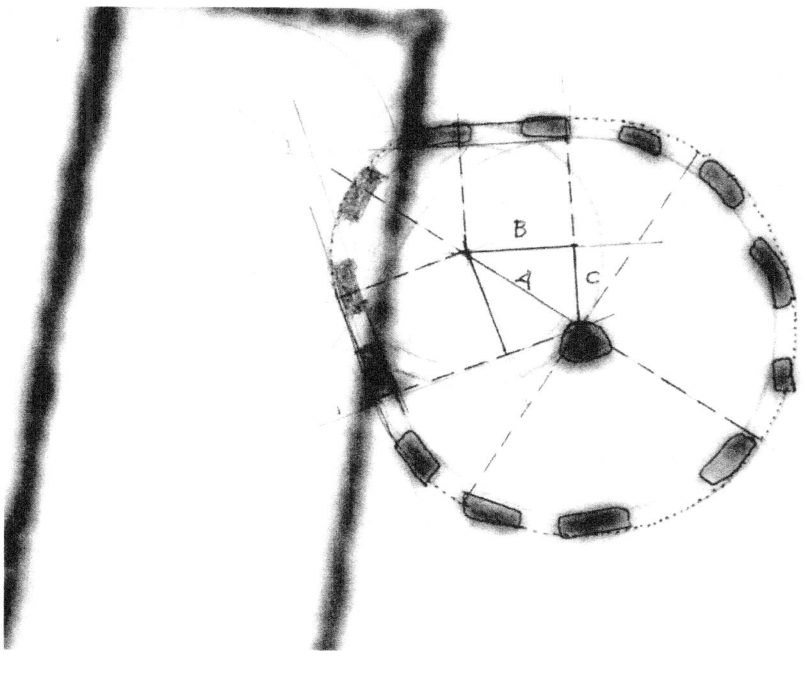

Figure 2S1   Needwood Farm Stone C

The 'circle' in fact is elongated and egg shaped about ~27 ft long by ~17 ft wide, an aspect ratio of ~8 : 5. This ratio is a commonly found Fibonacci integer convergent for the constant Phi. This was a considerable surprise. We note also that the egg is 27.05 ft on the long axis or 9.94 megalithic yards of 2.72 ft and 3.98 rods of 2.5 My. The width is 16.9 ft or 0.994 megalithic chains of 17 ft. We also have 101.3 ft / 16.9 ft = 5.994. The circle is 1 / 6 of an arc second across. This could all be coincidence but is suggestive. (To be complete we note that the length is 3.97 English rods and the circle d 1.025 English rods. As usual there is ambiguity because ancient metrics are related.) These are common metrics found on Late Neolithic and Bronze Age sites around Europe (6,1).

The presumed curb stones in fact appear to form a Type II Thom egg often found in Late Neolithic contexts in Britain and Europe (2). In lowland Cheshire stone circles are rare but not absent (5). Below we note cairn circles at Brickback Farm, Henbury, A) and Church Lawton III, B).

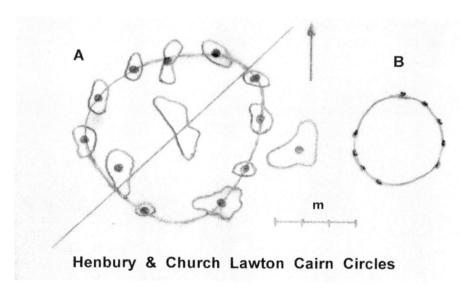

Henbury & Church Lawton Cairn Circles

At Henbury several large stones still exist in the fields but none is in position. The centres of the stone holes define a regular figure with an axis of symmetry and like Needwood, a central stone.

The figure is 22.4 ft long by 20.1 ft wide, comparable to Needwood. It appears to be an egg shaped circle but with a flattened, i.e. elliptical sw sector. The axis was measured *after* reconstruction. Its azimuth is ~47 degrees. The latitude of Brickback Farm is 53.254 N and working backwards cosine 53.254 x cosine 47 = sine 24.08. The axis points to mid summer sunrise and mid winter sunset. Henbury is in the same latitude band as our sites on Wirral, in fact the centre of the Burton Circle is at 53.258 N, the Two Mills row at 53.257 N and the Puddington stones at 53.257 N. Needwood stone A is at 53.32 N. Church Lawton III was a larger site with at least a dozen very large stones bordering a large earth mound between 22 and 23 metres in diameter.

It looks like another egg based on the remaining 9 standing stones. Of course we are assuming at Needwood that the 19th century OS surveyor took particular care to reproduce what he measured. There is though another strange coincidence. The egg construction triangle ABC has angles of approximately 37 : 90 : 53 degrees while the site latitude is 53.3 degrees north (but these proportions are also very close to a classic 3 : 4 : 5 Pythagorean construction triangle; see also Appendix 3. Very strangely the latitude of the Church Lawton circle is exactly right for a 3 : 4 : 5 construction triangle namely 53.1 d N).

This kind of geodetic symbolism is not uncommon in Britain and Europe (2, 6). Whatever the intention of the 'circle' it also appears to be *linked* to other site features. Its central stone forms a straight line with stone A and stone D. That seems beyond chance. The egg long axis is well defined at an azimuth of ~123 degrees. We can check to see if this has any astronomical or calendrical significance. Cos 123 x cos 53.34 = sine -18.98 degrees. The OOE ~2000 BC was 24 degrees. The declination of minor southern standstill moonrise of the moon in its 18.6 year nodal cycle was on average -24 + 5.1 = -18.9 degrees. The angle was measured *after* the axis was reconstructed. We seem to have a collection of coincidences involving the 'cairn' which are hard to explain by chance. In megalithic architecture, figure construction lines often point to sol-lunar horizon events (2). Perhaps this is just another coincidence but the probability of a chance hit is 0.083 – 0.167. Stone A also appears to be the locus for several interesting lines as we will see.

Stone C, comparing OS maps, Google Maps and aerial photos is still in its original position. Its basic form is of rectangular cross section but with a curved concave surface on the east side (Figure 2S1). The stone is heavily weathered. A few 'slots' appear on the stone, a common fate of standing stones, but there are no 18th / 19th century iron hinges which often also appear on ancient standing stones. Recently somebody has unfortunately incised a circle into the stone of the west face along with a painted blue cross. There are also several small well defined circular holes on the north face. The upper east face has a regular triangular, hoof shaped, cut depression, centrally placed with one vertex pointing upwards. The form is clearly man made (Figure 2S2). This east face curiously, matches the shape of Wirral! We also note that another stone appears to have survived in situ. This is stone B now behind a high fence in scrub woodland in the Mount Road Recycling Centre. This stone also deserves a careful appraisal.

Stone D is interesting since on the 25 inch maps it is shown as having an elongated vertical cross section rather than as a point. It must have been a very large stone. The author has found only several sandstone fragments at the location.

There is also a dump of large sandstone pillars in the woods to the north but some of these are clearly left from the demolition of a large 19th century house, 'Brakenwood'. Some stones left there are rougher and deserve further attention since several ancient stones were removed from the Needwood Farm site and the M53 motorway works area in 1970-71. Figure 1 shows us other interesting features. The farm seems to favour calendrical arrangements of boundaries. The western boundary of the farm follows the old Mount Road and has two stones A and F. That boundary is due north – south, a meridian line. The farm lane from Brimstage Road is also due north – south as is field boundary FB2 (and its line extended also crosses stone H2 at Clatterbridge: see Figure 3, below).

Field boundary FB1 is also due east – west, an equinox line. The line AC coincides with the junction of FB1 and the N-S farm lane. This encourages a closer look at the farm boundaries. The 19th century Urban District and civil parish boundary crosses the farm in the south east. Did it respect an earlier marked, traditional boundary?

Figure 2S2   Stone C East Face

A ~80 degree sector here is defined by an accurate circular arc. The centre of that arc is at point O, among the farm buildings. This could be coincidence. However that centre lies on the due north – south farm lane meridian discussed above.

We also note that stones B and C sit on the *same* circular arc with a centre also at O. That is a multiple coincidence. Here is another. Using the NLS mapping tools the radius of the proposed boundary circle, R1, is ~658 ft. The radius of the arc through B and C, R2, is ~406 ft. The ratio of the radii is therefore 658 / 406 = 1.62 but Phi = 1.618. Here is another strange feature. The author routinely checks for signs of geodetic and ancient metrics. We note that here, 406 ft is also 406 / 101.3 = 4.008 arc seconds and 658 ft is 658 / 101.3 = 6.496 or closely 6.5 arc seconds. 406 ft is 23.9 megalithic chains. If 6.5 / 4 *was* intended the ratio is 1.625 = 13 / 8 which is a Fibonacci integer convergent for Phi. Earlier we noted the 8 / 5 convergent in the proportions of the proposed cairn circle. This is another peculiar coincidence. Note also that the radius of the BC arc is ~406 ft and the cairn circle length ~27.05 ft. Their size ratio is 15.01, closely integer. Curiously 406 / 16.9 = 24.02 and 658 / 16.9 = 38.93, closely integer. Perhaps we should check other site inter-stone distances?

AB	~713 ft	7.04 arc seconds	ACairn	~1111 ft	10.97 arc seconds
AC	~1010 ft	9.97	AO	~1114 ft	11.0
AD	~923 ft	9.10	AF	~508 ft	5.015

In Figure 3 we also note AS: ~1624 ft; 16.03 arc seconds. Summing this sample of A based lines we get 69.12 arc seconds. The integer error is 0.18%. This is remarkable. Discounting the author's insanity these measurements imply that the 'builders', of whatever date, used a metric very close to the modern arc second or ~101.3 ft or some sub-unit of it. However early metrics are often related so ambiguity is common as noted earlier. For example we noted the cairn circle length as ~10 My of 2.72 ft and width ~16.9 ft. But a megalithic chain is 17 ft while an English rod is 16.5 ft. Note also that 16.64 ft is 5 metres of 3.281 ft and an arc second / 6 = 101.3 / 6 = 16.88 ft.

The metre was geodetically defined two hundred years ago but perhaps earlier cultures did the same with related metrics (see Appendices 1 & 2). The distance O to cairn circle centre is ~81.3 ft and 11.96 megalithic rods and 29.9 megalithic yards and 0.802 ~ 4 / 5 arc seconds.

Figure 3   Brakenwood & Clatterbridge Area

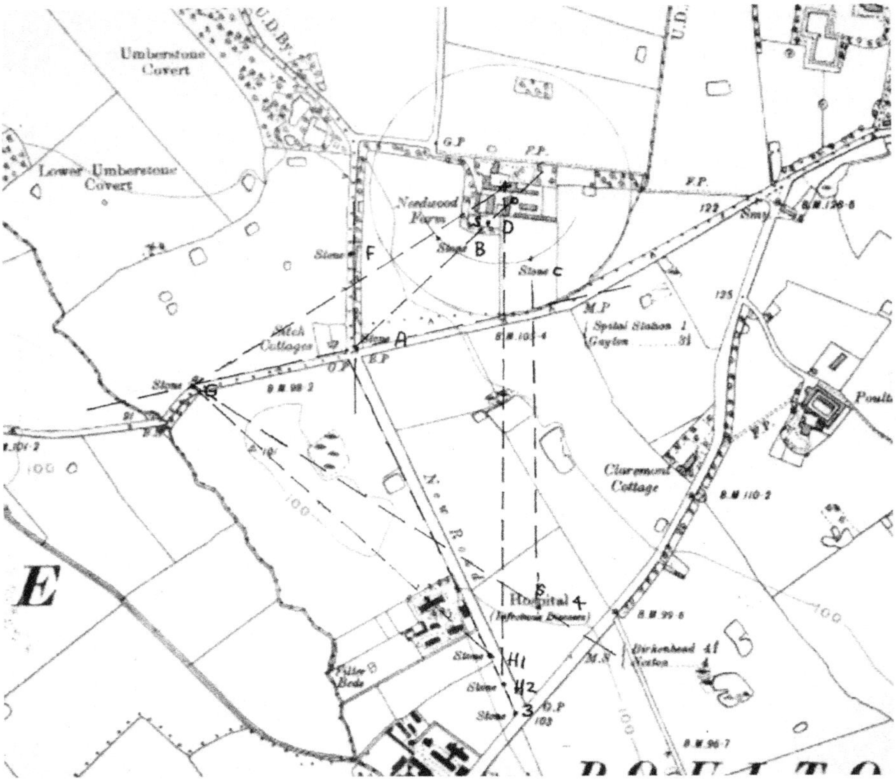

A3.2   Stone G and the Clatterbridge Stones

We should now consider other stones in the nearby area which may be connected to the Brakenwood site (see Figure 3). We noted stone G which sits to the west of A on Brimstage Road. Here are some inter-stone distances involving G.

GA ~ 836 ft 8.25 arc seconds   GB ~1468 ft   14.49 arc seconds
     (122.94 MR)   (215.9 MR)
GC   1827 ft 18.04 "   "   GCairn 1877 ft 18.48 "   "
     (107.5 MR)   (276.03 MR)
GF   1065 ft 10.51 "   "   GO   1857 ft 18.332 "   "
                                 (273.09 MR)

Four lines are integer in Meg Rods.
Curiously GF / GA = 1065 / 836 = 1.274 = Pi / 4 = √ Phi.

We turn to the cluster of stones near Clatterbridge Hospital. H1 – H3 stand on what is now Mount Road. However on the Bryant map of 1831 this was known as Broad Lane. Stone H2 is due south of the meridian Needwood Farm lane and also our proposed circle centre at O. The distances to the H stones are again interesting.

OH1	~2440 ft	24.08 arc seconds	OH2	~2581 ft	25.48 arc seconds
	(358.8 MR)			(151.83 MC)	
OH3	2734 ft	26.98	GH3	2335 ft	23.05
	(402.06 MR)				
GS	2075 ft	20.48	CS	1821 ft	17.98
	(305.1 MR)			(107.1 MC)	

Of the 12 distances considered, 10 use megalithic units and 8 appear to be set out in MRs. The H stones are equally spaced by 1.5 arc seconds and we have several integer or ½ arc second multiples as we do for the G distances to stones. This suggests the stones identified across the area may be related. We already noted the meridian lines AF, CS, OH2, FB2, the equinox line FB1 and the linear AH1H2H3 line along the old Mount Road (the Broad Lane of 1831). Having found interesting patterns in layout and dimensions the next question is: do the stone patterns have any calendrical or astronomical significance?

A3.3   Astronomical Alignments

Note again that the long axis of the cairn circle had an azimuth of ~123 degrees and a declination of -19 degrees which marks the most southerly rising point of the moon at minor standstill in the nodal cycle, nominally in the Late Neolithic. However a millennium ago the azimuth would be little changed at ~122 degrees and precision on the map is not guaranteed. Also horizon elevation is raised to the north east of the site, delaying moonrise compared to theory while refraction would advance moonrise significantly. Even so the fit is close. So we begin with the cairn itself and stone A where a number of lines cross.

The azimuth of A-D-Cairn is ~47 degrees and the declination cos 47 x cos 53.34 = sin 24.03 degrees. This of course is the declination of midsummer sunrise circa 2000 BC but the azimuth in Saxon times would be ~47.7 degrees, hardly distinguishable given map recording / reading accuracy. We have a 3 point linear line here suggesting intention. If so the chance probability of hitting one of our 15 horizon target azimuths is 0.0833 – 0.167 depending on the target width assumption (1 or 2 degrees). Note also that the reciprocal direction from the cairn to A in the south west is 303 degrees, the direction of midwinter sunset. If the cairn circle marked a burial perhaps both directions are of importance, signaling death (midwinter sunset) and resurrection (midsummer sunrise). D was a large stone giving a good back sight to both the cairn circle and A fore sights. The same dual situation holds at Stonehenge and a century of archaeological debate has not settled the matter.

On Merseyside the author has discovered a number of sites where the midwinter sunset *was* marked, most notably at the Calderstones passage grave in Liverpool and, probably, at a site on Vineyard Farm ridge, Poulton Lancelyn (section 9). Of course we may simply have yet another strange coincidence. Let us look then at the line AC. The azimuth is ~69 degrees and the declination 12.3 degrees but this is the solar declination midway between the spring equinox and midsummer solstice at 12 d with an azimuth of 69.6 degrees. We can also look at the midway azimuth which is (47.06 + 90) / 2 = 68.5 degrees. So line AC marks the mean of (68.5 + 69.6) / 2 = 69.05 degrees. Another coincidence. The line F- Cairn is also close at azimuth ~67 degrees.

The line AB is interesting at ~37 degrees azimuth giving a declination of 28.6 degrees. However the moon at northerly major standstill had a declination of 24 + 5.1 = 29.1 degrees and an azimuth of 36 degrees.

The angle AO has an azimuth of 42 degrees and a declination of 26.34 degrees but the midway point between northern major lunar standstill and the mean east west, equinox, rising point is (29.1 + 24) / 2 = 26.55 d. There are several other possible 2 stone lines we should record.

AF has 0 d azimuth, a meridian line.

A-Circle centre has declination 25.9 d v (29.1 + 24) / 2 = 26.55 d

So A-D-Cairn, A –C centre, A-B form a set marking the interval from extreme northern moonrise to summer solstice / moonrise midpoint.

F-B declination 5.34 d v 5.14 d marking northern equinox moonrise

F-C declination -5.36 d v -5.14 d " southern " "

These lines centred on F, form a matched pair. Chance is unlikely.

F-D declination 6.5 d and 19 / 3 = 6.33 d, 1 / 3 way moonrise point ?

B-C declination - 9 d v - (19 + 0) /2 = - 9.5 d, moonrise midpoint ?

O-C declination -33.5 d v – 33 d extreme southern Venus declination point

What about using stone G as a back sight?

GO azimuth 57 degrees;   northerly minor standstill rising
        declination 19 d   of the moon declination at 18.9 d

GC azimuth 70 degrees;   mid declination sunrise between
summer
        declination 11.8 d   solstice and equinox is 12 d

GA azimuth 77.5 degrees;   2 / 3 way point sunrise between
summer
        declination 7.4 d   solstice and equinox at declination
8 d ?

Now we come to a cluster of close azimuths involving stone G.

GB   azimuth 59 d; declination 17.9 d

G-Cairn azimuth 60 d; declination 17.4 d   Mean declination
17.37 d

GD   azimuth 61 d; declination 16.8 d

GB and GD are symmetrical in azimuth and declination about the G-Cairn line. This looks like intent but why? The 60 : 90 : 30 triangle of course has long known and special geometrical properties e.g. that tan 60 = $\sqrt{3}$ and sin 60 = $\sqrt{3}$ / 2.

These proportions seem to crop up in the architecture of many periods most notably in the arch design of medieval cathedral windows as the Vesica Piscis, the Bladder of the Fish, but it also occurs widely in megalithic stone circles. However there is another calendrical link. A sunrise azimuth of 60 d occurs ~47 days after the spring equinox on about May 5th. This is a true temporal midpoint or 'cross quarter' day between equinox and summer solstice. A sunrise azimuth of 61 d occurs ~43 days after the equinox which takes us approximately to May 1st, May Day, and the ancient feast of Beltaine. We cannot know the builders' intent but both the true astronomical 'cross quarter' day and the ancient May festival are marked in these stones. That is most impressive.

Now we look to the stones at Clatterbridge using G as a backsight.

GS   azimuth 123 d; declination -18.98 d   moonrise at southern
                                                minor standstill

GH1 azimuth 132 d; declination -23.7 d   winter solstice sunrise
?

GH2 azimuth 134 d ; declination -24.5 d

GH3 azimuth 136 d ; declination -25.4 d

Mean GH1/2 azimuth 133 d, declination - 24.05 d

D-H2 azimuth zero, meridian line.

GS is the minor standstill point in the lunar nodal cycle familiar from other places. The GH lines seem to be related to winter solstice sunrise at -24 d declination. GH1 – GH2 bracket the sunrise. GH3 is beyond the sun's range. However the moon at mid nodal cycle passes through -24 d on its way to the major southern standstill at declination -29 d. The H stones would enable the maximum speed of the moon through declination -24 to be estimated. However this would imply rather sophisticated monitoring. GH1/2 it is certain, marked sunrise at the winter solstice and GS marked moonrise at southern minor standstill. We found earlier that GO marked the northern minor standstill point.

Note also

S-H1 declination 25 d v 24 d summer solstice sunrise
S-H2 declination 33 d v 32-33 d extreme Venus declination north
S-H3 declination 35.8 d, possible stellar rise point seen in other places?

At Needwood we have only one three point line A-D-Cairn at declination 24 d marking summer solstice sunrise. That appears to be intentional. Other possible lines here have only two points although we have sets of lines from the same origin which appear to mark the approach to or straddle key horizon events. To calculate the chance probabilities here we must consider all possible combinations of two stones. Altogether we have 10 stones plus an inferred circle centre and the cairn. We leave out the cairn since its date is uncertain. The number of possible stone pairs is then 11 x 10 / 2 = 55. The number of hits in terms of the 15 major targets we originally identified is 11. The possible routes to 11 hits with 55 pairs is

$$C(11) = 55! / (11! \times (55 - 11)!) = 1.2 \times 10^{11}$$

So chance probability is given by

$$(1/12)^{11} \times (11/12)^{44} \times 1.2 \times 10^{11} = 3.51 \times 10^{-3} \quad \text{Chance is eliminated.}$$

It could be argued that G, S and the H stones are not part of the Needwood complex. Suppose we consider only the immediate farm site? We then have 5 stones and the circle centre. There are 15 possible 2 point lines. Checking we find there are 6 definite hits on our 15 item, original target list so the number of routes is

$$C(6) = 15! / (6! \times (15 - 6)!) = 5.0 \times 10^{3} \quad \text{and probability is}$$

$$(1/12)^{6} \times (11/12)^{9} \times 5 \times 10^{3} = 7.65 \times 10^{-4}. \quad \text{Chance is again eliminated.}$$

The author tried various draconian culls of the lines observed but still found chance strongly rejected. These clear, unambiguous astronomical results alone are remarkable in relation to the Brakenwood – Clatterbridge standing stone field. The implication is that we have a major observation site of the Late Neolithic or Bronze Age here.

The only other explanation is a mad (but extremely knowledgeable), 'Druid' obsessed, on the level, antiquarian landowner of the 18th or 19th century mimicking ancient alignments. We could draw the same conclusion for several other sites since the results are repeatedly surprising. We will notice later that a few ancient Wirral family names keep cropping up. Let the reader decide on the 'mad landowner' hypothesis having studied all the sites and Appendix 3.

Appendix 4   Irby Site 1

Irby is an area with evidence of occupation from several periods. A Romano-British farmstead was excavated near the village with evidence of an earlier settlement, possibly Bronze Age, beneath the later site. There is a Roman well to the west on a footpath to Thurstaston. In the east near Harrock Wood are several tithe fields called Autons. This is a version of the Saxon, Aughton or Acton which indicated a meeting site or moot, the equivalent of Thingwall, the Norse Thing site, a mile or so to the east. To the west of the Arrowe Brook are three large fields including 'Heskeths' in their names. This is the Norse, *hestaskeid*, a horse racing track. At the west end of the village is Irby Hall in a medieval moated enclosure surrounded by clear medieval field ridge and furrow lines on the Lidar image.

The author took an interest in Irby for two reasons. Firstly, it is on a western escape route from the Battlefield of Brunanburh around Clatterbridge, through Thingwall and Norse held territory to the coast at Dawpool where Irish ships could take off the defeated army of Anlaf. Secondly, Saxon 'Acton' sites were often based on far earlier meeting places. It seemed an obvious area for possible Bronze Age or Neolithic feature but old OS maps showed little.

By chance the author scanned the area near Harrock Wood at the maximum scale on the current OS online maps and a pattern of 10 stones suddenly appeared (see below). It was immediately obvious that the stones were arranged in sets of 3 along 4 very accurate straight lines. The stones did not relate to the old tithe field boundaries except at s6. The first thought was that these were once marker stones for the Viking horse race track, the hestaskeid.

Stones 6, 7, 8, 9 were indeed on the eastern edge of tithe fields named 'Heskeths & Backside' and 'Part of Heskeths but other Hesketh fields lay further west, towards Irby Village. Stones 5, C, 1, 2, 3, 4 are not on Hesketh named fields. Stones 1, 2, 3, 4 lie on tithe fields involving 'Autons' names, signifying a Saxon and possibly earlier moot site.

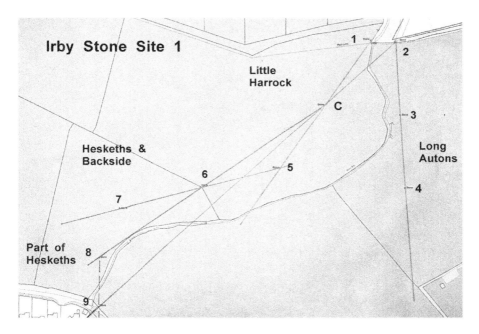

As in all these analyses the test lies in the geometrical properties of the stone lines, on the assumption that Viking horsemen and Saxon landsmen were not into complex geometry and astronomy. What follows on this site has surprised and disturbed the author more than any other site on Wirral. The first point is the accuracy with which the 3 stones forming each line were laid out. Lines several hundred feet long are dead straight.

The second point is: the probability of 10 stones arranging themselves into 5, accurate 3 stone lines, by chance is negligible. The third point is three of the lines pass through the same point, sC and two lines pass through s2, s5 and s6. This stone layout was an intentional design, clearly having nothing to do with boundary definition. Next we examine the dimensions of the lines in relation to the possible metrics used and the proportions of the lines.

s1s2 is ~40.45 ft; 14.9 megalithic yards; 5.95 meg chains; 0.4 arc seconds; 2.45 English rods.

s1sCs5 is ~261.4 ft; 96.1 meg yard; 38.44 meg rods; 2.58 arc seconds; 15.84 English rods.
s1sC = sCs5 ~130.7 ft; 48.05 meg yards; 19.2 meg rods; 7.92 English rods.
s5s6 is 134.8 ft; 49.57 meg yards; 19.8 meg rods; 4 / 3 arc seconds; 8.2 English rods.
s6s7 is 137.4 ft; 50.5 meg yards; 20.2 meg rods; 8.08 meg chains; 8.3 English rods.
s5s6s7 is 272.2 ft; 100.07 meg yards; 40.03 meg rods; 16.01 meg chains; 16.5 English rods.
It seems likely that the builders intended s5s6 = s6s7.

s2s3s4 is 248.2 ft; 91.2 meg yards; 36.5 meg rods; 2.45 arc seconds; 15.04 English rods.
s2s3 = s3s4 is 124.1 ft; 45.6 meg yards; 18.25 meg rods; 1.225 arc seconds = $\sqrt{3}/\sqrt{2}$; 7.52 English rods.

s6sCs8 is 452.6 ft; 166.4 ft; 61.17 meg yards; 24.48 meg rods; 4.47 arc seconds; 27.42 English rods.
s6s8 is 202ft ; 74.26 meg yards; 29.7 meg rods; 11.9 meg chains; 1.994 arc seconds; 12.24 English rods.

sCs6 is 250.6 ft; 92.1 meg yards; 36.86 meg rods; 2.47 arc seconds; 15.19 English rods. We have ~2, 2.5, 4.5 arc seconds but the closest match is in meg rods : 24.5, 30, 37. We see that

$$30 / 37 = 0.81 = 1.62 / 2; \quad 24.5 / 37 = 0.662 = (0.813)^2 = (1.626 / 2)^2$$

We seem to have an exercise in Phi proportions in the design. 1.625 is the Fibonacci Phi convergent 13 / 8. The longest line has the most extreme proportions, s2sCs9. Was there geometrical intention behind this?

s2sCs9 is 658.9 ft; 242.2 meg yards; 96.9 meg rods; 38.76 meg chains; 6.503 arc seconds; 39.93 English rods.
s2sC is 155.2 ft; 57.06 meg yards; 22.82 meg rods; 9.12 meg chains; 1.53 arc seconds; 9.4 English rods.
sCs9 is 503.7 ft; 185.18 meg yards; 74.07 meg rods; 4.97 arc seconds; 30.53 English rods.

Note that we also have ~ 6.5, 5, 1.5 arc second lengths. The line proportions are very interesting and familiar.

$$97 / 74 = 1.3108 = 2.621 / 2 = (1.619)^2 / 2.$$ We know that Phi = 1.618 but also that the Fibonacci convergent, 34 / 21 = 1.619. Also

$$97 / 23 = 4.218 = (1.616)^3 \qquad 74 / 23 = 3.22 = 1.61 \times 2$$

We have 5 lines laid out in integer megalithic metrics with 3 lines divided as 1 : 1 and 2 lines in simple Phi proportions. This is the most transparent piece of geometrical scaling so far discovered on the Wirral. We also note that this array was deliberately designed by someone who knew the Golden Section and its significance. Finally note that the circle with centre s3 passing though s2 and s4 also passes through sC. Circles passing through s7 and s5 (centred on s6) and through s1 and s5 (centred on sC) cross at s5. (These two circle intersection points define a line of 145 d azimuth, -29.3 d declination, extreme southern moonrise at major standstill).

What about general astronomy at Irby? We have five 3 stone lines which are clearly intentional and some obvious 2 stone lines. Working from west to east :

s7s6s5 azimuth 75 d, declination 8.9 d. ? (24 +0) / 3 = 8d, 1/3 way sunrise?

s8s6sC azimuth 56 d, dec 19.5 d; moonrise at northern minor standstill has dec 19.13 d.

s9sCs2 azimuth 47 d, dec 24.05 d; summer solstics sunrise is at 24 d declination.

s5sCs1 azimuth 34 d, dec 29.6 d; moonrise at northern major standstill has dec 29.13 d.

s4s3s2 azimuth ~358 d, dec 36.6 d; this is not quite a meridian line but could mark the setting azimuth of a bright, nearly circumpolar star as we have noted at several sites. The pole of the sky at this latitude would be at 36.68 d altitude. A quick check shows that s9s8 is an accurate meridian line. Also s6s4 is a good equinox line. sCs4 has an azimuth of 132 d , declination -23. 6 d, close to winter solstice sunrise, matching s9sCs2 summer solstice line, both events being observable from sC. From sC both rising and setting events would be observable. What about a chance explanation? We have three, 3 stone lines with obvious, *major* solar – lunar events. The ~9 d line could be a 1/3 way sunrise marker displaced by horizon elevation. We have one probable stellar line seen at several sites but that was not in our initial target set. So we call 3 hits out of 5.

$$(1 / 12)^3 \times (11 / 12)^2 \times 5! / (3! \, 2!) = 4.86 \times 10^{-3} \text{ or 1 in 206.}$$

These are good odds, from the astronomy alone, in favour of deliberate intention. We also noted some transparent, very significant two stone alignments supporting intent.

As an old engineer and astronomer, my sense is that Irby 1 was about clever surveying and manipulating symbolic geometry, with a nod to the key solar and lunar events only. This was not a site for the detailed, technical study, of sol-lunar movements which appears to be the case elsewhere. I have a strong sense of a canny designer really enjoying himself while telling his chieftain that his geometrical 'earth magic' will please the gods and help the crops grow. Of course I am assuming that the stone array is ancient. Its local Irby context certainly is.

Even so, we must still consider a modern (19th century) hoax, with 'Druid' obsessed landowners (of ancient lineage) somehow able to tap into a genuine 'Masonic' body of knowledge to create their landscape follies across Wirral.

Appendix 5   Birkenhead

Birkenhead does not seem like a promising area to seek out Neolithic or Bronze Age remains since by the mid 19th century the town was already well developed. However, looking carefully at the early 6 inch OS maps and the tithe maps is revealing. We begin with Birkenhead Park. In the south west in the vicinity of Park Drive and Ashville Road there was once a possible barrow cemetary with several 'burial mounds' known as The Bonks (22). A bonk is a blow to the head in ME. However we also have bank, hill and in ON, banki. Is this a genuine Norse name survival on Ufaldi's land? It is said that children once rolled decorated hard boiled eggs down the barrows at Easter, an ancient tradition. Were the Bonks late Neolithic or Bronze Age remains?

The area on the old tithe field maps is transected by Lowfields Lane. Lowe is a recognized term for a burial mound. The mounds are not clear now. On Ashville Road (by the cricket club) there is still a high ridge of land cut through by the road. However the situation is complicated by possible landscaping activities further east. In some places we can still see low conical mounds of a respectable size, usually among the trees. Is this 19th century landscaping? Were all the mounds merely landscaping? The Bonks were unique on Wirral and perhaps they point to a Neolithic settlement here with access to the Mersey and the Irish Sea via Wallasey Pool. The Calderstones passage grave and other remains in Liverpool prove the early local links to Ireland. We noted earlier that several such barrow cemeteries are known in Cheshire.

What would confirm the early date of these mounds is the presence of standing stones and indeed there were a surprising number on the site and in the areas not far to the south, to the west and to the north. Current online, large scale OS maps, remarkably, still show 12 standing stone positions with 2 on Ashville Road and 10 to the east. On some 19th century OS maps a few of the stones are marked as B.S. This is not unusual.

The designations come and go over the decades. The current online map does not use B.S. but 'stone', the usual modern name for ancient markers. The test is how the stones are, or are not, geometrically related and orientated as we will see.

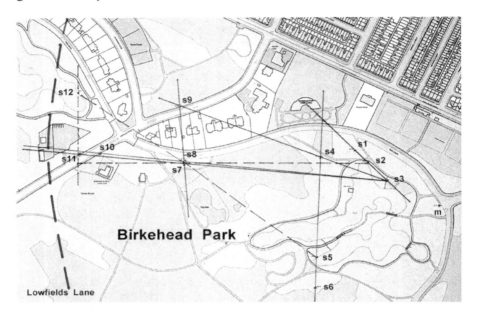

Nearby, to the west, on Park Road North on the 1872 6 inch OS map, three standing stones stood in a triangular arrangement at the edge of the Park. A circle of ~40 ft diameter can be drawn through the stones. Lowfields Lane passed close to the western Park stones and another stood on it at the junction with Park Road North.

To the north, beyond Upper Beckwirth St. stood a cluster of at least nine standing stones, some of which helped define the new roads in the area as Birkenhead developed. Strangely Lowfields Lane heads directly north to join Beckwith St. To the east another group of at least 5 stones stood between Cleveland St and Corporation Road. Other stones stood along the south bank of Wallasey Pool.

Birkenhead deserves close study in its own right. Below we take a preliminary look at Birkenhead Park. We have 12 stones recorded in the park plus stone m which is a 19th century stone memorial. We also note 10 good straight lines consisting of at least 3 stones each.

s1s2s3 s2s7s8 s3s4s9 s3s8s10   s3s7s8s11 s4s5s6 s7s8s9
s5s7s8 s6s7s8   s7s8s12

We can say immediately that the probability of having 12 stones arrange themselves into 10 accurate lines of 3 stones, by chance, is minute. We can also check out the line horizon azimuths as usual, looking to the eastern, rising sector.

s1s2s3 azimuth 134 d; declination -24.5 d ; winter solstice sunrise is at -24.0 declination

s2s7s8 azimuth 90 d; dec 0 d ; equinox sunrise and sunset

s3s4s9 azimuth 110 d; dec -11.8 d ; equinox / winter solstice mid declination sunrise -12 d.

s3s8s10   azimuth 95 d; dec -3 d   ?

s3s7s8s11   azimuth 93.3 d; dec – 2.1 d   ?

s4s5s6   azimuth 3 d ; 36.6 dec   star rise ?

s7s8s9   azimuth 356 d ; 36.6 dec   star set ?

s6s7s8   azimuth 133 d; dec -24.1 d; winter solstice sunrise -24 d dec.

s7s8s12 azimuth 123 d; dec – 19 d; moonrise at southern minor standstill
s5s7s8   azimuth 126 d ; dec -20.6 d   "   "   "   "   "

Six of these 3 stone azimuths are very familiar giving major solar and lunar horizon events including equinox sunrise at dec 0 d. But we also have s3s7s8s11 and s3s8s10 with declinations -2.1 d and -3 d. These are part way to southern extreme equinox moonrise at declination -5.13 d. We have stones 3, 7, 8, 10, 11 all lying close to similar lines. In fact s10s7 has a measured declination of - 4.8 d. This related sub-set of stones is therefore well suited to tracking the zone of 0 declination (mean equinox) to – 5.13 d declination (lunar extreme southern equinox position).

The moon again seems to be of great interest. If so we are missing one major position: moonrise at southern major standstill at declination -29.1 d. However s6s9 has a declination of -28.9 d. We also note s6s10 has a declination of -19 d matching that of s7s8s12 and marking moonrise at southern minor standstill. For completeness note that s11s12 marks an accurate meridian line. We assume that long, accurate 3 stone lines were intentionally laid out. Looking only at the 3 stone lines we can readily accept 5 clear, solar / lunar alignments.

The 3, 7, 8,10, 11 subset we will accept as monitoring the 0 d to -5 d declination lunar equinox range and count the subset as one hit. That gives us 6 hits from 10 lines. The probability of any stone line matching one of the 15 major solar / lunar events we took as 1 / 12 (allowing a 1 d wide target) so the probability of what we see in Birkenhead Park occurring by chance is

$$(1 / 12)^6 \times (11 / 12)^4 \times 10! / (6! \times 4!) = 4.95 \times 10^{-5}.$$

Let us be even more rigorous in our interpretation. Stones 7 and 8 are close together and an implicit assumption above is that they acted as a narrow foresight for several alignments. Suppose we treat them as a single stone position. This reduces the number of acceptable 3 stone lines to 4 but all align with major events.

The chance probability then becomes 4.8×10^{-5}, similar good odds for an intentional stone arrangement. The two remaining 3 stones lines, s4s5s6 and s7s8s9 straddle the meridian line symmetrically, having identical declinations.

All we can say is they could mark the rising and setting points of an almost circumpolar, bright star at the time of construction. Around 2500 BC three bright stars are possible : Deneb (Alpha Cygni), Beta Leonis and Alpha Cassiopeiae. Deneb is the brightest star and had a steady declination for many centuries around 1500 BC – 2500 BC. It is interesting that we have seen similar apparent stellar declinations at other Wirral sites including Carlett Park and Eastham. We may be seeing the marking of so-called 'clock stars' here. On the early tithe field maps we noted two additional stones on Lowfields Lane. Stone X was just west of s12, a position now in the lake. Stone Y was at the junction of Lowfields Lane and Cleveland Street.

Are these missing stones related to the marked stones in the Park? Well sXs12s9 forms a good straight line of azimuth ~98.5 d, declination - 5 d. It is closely parallel to the main east – west stones apparently marking the southern equinox moonrise at declination - 5.13 d. We may consider this a smoking gun. Stone Y forms an accurate meridian line with s10 and is parallel to s11s12 nearby. We also note that sYs4 has an azimuth of 133 d, declination -24 d. It is parallel to line s1s2s3 nearby. This appears to be another smoking gun. A third stone was eventually found on the faded tithe field map just north of the current Park Road South, adjacent to Park High School eastern boundary.

Stone Z is due south of s9 so that sZs9 is an accurate meridian line.This could of course be a coincidence. However we also note that sZ forms a straight line sXs11sZ with stone X also found on the old tithe maps. The azimuth of sXs11sZ is 158 d, declination – 33.6 d. This is close to the extreme southern risng point of Venus at declination -33 d which we have met before. Finally sZs6 has an azimuth of 46 d, declination 24.4 d compared with mid-summer sunrise at declination 24 d. These latter results make the point that all stones are not marked on all maps and that some stone positions must be lost. It is therefore the more remarkable that any consistent patterns remain.

The stones of Upper Beckwith St. are also of great interest with apparent regular geometrical layouts and associated horizon alignments. Six stones appear to lie on a pair of concentric circles with a centre at C. The two inner circle stones share a line with an outer circle stone, giving s1s3s5. Stones 2 and 4 are also close to this main 'axis'.This geometry is highly unlikely to have occured by chance. We can add to this, the properties of the two outer circle stones s9 and s10 which are far from the main 'axis'. However the line s9s10 is also at a right angle to the axis line mid(s1s2)s3sC which bisects s9s10. The points sC, s9, s10 form a good equilateral triangle enclosed in the large circle. (Enclosed equilateral triangles are also present in the proposed Overchurch and Arrowe Park circles; 1). This is clearly a deliberate construction which we will show is related to the horizon astronomy.

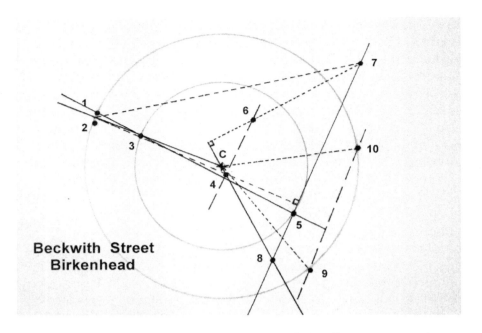

Beckwith Street Birkenhead

We can also note that s9s10 is closely parallel to line s8s5s7 and to line s4s6. S4s6 and s8s5s7 are therefore also at a right angle to 'axis' line. These three north-northeast trending lines share a highly significant horizon declination (see below). S7 joined to s1, s2 also forms right triangles with the 'axis' stones. The triangle with sides s7s1 and s1s4(8,5,7 intersection) and s7(8,5,7 intersection) has angles of ~53.5, ~90 and ~36.5 degrees. Our site latitude is 53.4 d north. Recall also that the ubiquitous Neolithic 'circle' forming triangle, 3: 4: 5 has angles 53.1, 90, 36.9 d.

Finally, we note a third obvious right triangle with sides based on lines s6s7, sCs4s8 and line s8s5s7. The angle at s8 is ~51 d and at s7 ~39 d. This, remarkably, is also a familiar triangle from Stonehenge and other megalithic sites. We see that

$\tan(38.97) = 0.809 = \text{Phi}/2$ $\sin(38.97) = 0.6289 = 1/1.59$

We noted earlier our two hypothetical, concentric construction circles. The ratio of their diameters is ~1.587 so the triangle and the circles are directly related. The triangle sides have the proportions Phi : 2 : 1.59 Phi.

So we have an equilateral triangle, a triangle recording the site latitude of 53.4 d and a Phi related triangle, all based on the circles. This is quite an impressive geometrical exercise which must have been premeditated. But was it purely an exercise? Let us examine the horizon alignments of the 3 stone (and some clearly related 2 stone) lines.

s8s5s7   azimuth 25 d declination 32.7 d; Venus extreme declination
32-33 d

s9s10   azimuth 24 d dec 33.0 d

s4s6   azimuth 25.5 dec 32.5 d

As on other Wirral sites we have a clear pointer to extreme Venus rising. The other option is a bright star rising point. In 2500 BC we have only Alpha Cassiopeiae; in 2000 BC Beta Leonis. But also we have
sCs4s8 azimuth ~153 d   dec -32 d; Venus extreme southern rising - 33 d.
The main 'axis' stones yield a number of close horizon azimuths.
s1s2s5   azimuth 117.5 d dec -16 d; Venus extreme -32.5 / 2 = - 16.25 d
s1s2s5 appears to mark the mid declination point beween extreme southern rising and the equinox rising line.

The two stone line s6s7 is also of interest providing a matching northern declination.
s6s7 azimuth 62 d dec 16.25; Venus extreme 32.5 / 2 = 16.25 d

The line mid(s1s2)s3s4 is also closely at a right angle to our long Venus line s8s5s7. Mid(s1s2)s3s4   azimuth 115 d dec -14.6 d; but - 14.6 = -29.2 / 2, marking the mid declination point beween the equinox and the extreme southern moonrise point at major standstill at declination -29.13 d.

s2s7 and s4s10 *may* also be lunar related lines since
s2s7, s4s10 azimuths 77 - 78d   dec 7.4 d; but 29.13 / 4 = 7.3 d
We also have s1s10 giving
s1s10 azimuth 99 d dec -5.3 d; extreme southern equinox
moonrise -5.13 d

The only major solar alignments are s4s9 azimuth ~132 d dec -23.5 d and close by sCs9, azimuth 133 d dec -24 d which mark midwinter sunrise at declination -24 d. We have four good, 3 stone lines with significant horizon events. However we did not include Venus mid-declination events in our original horizon set so we count 3 out of 4 horizon event hits at Beckwith Street. The probability of 3 chance hits is then

$$(1/12) \times (11/12)^3 \times 4!/3! = 2.1 \times 10^{-3}$$ and odds of 1 to 471.

The several obvious, good, two stone hits related to Venus and the moon also give informal support. We can also see now the significance of some of the site geometrical features. The right triangle based on s6s7, s4s8 and s8s5s7, tells us that the extreme southern rising of Venus is at a right angle to the the mid way declination between extreme northern rising and the equinox rising. That is Az 62.5 d and declination 16 d or 32/2 d is at right angles to az (62.5+90) and declination -32 d. This relationship holds for any latidude but only at our latitude do the azimuths 62.5 d and 152.5 d hold. To see both angles together suggests at least empirical intent by the builders. To see the geometrical constructions here, further suggests understanding among the designers. This modest stone site teaches many lessons if we look closely. Earlier we noted the ratio of the construction circle diameters but did not give the actual dimensions. Here they are, scaled from the 1872 6 inch OS map. Large circle diameter 1,639.7 ft; 99.34 English rods; 241.1 Megalithic rods. Small circle diameter 1,033.4 ft; 62.63 English rods; 151.97 Megalithic rods. Both diameters are integer multiples of Thom's megalithic rod. 241 / 152 = $\sqrt{(5/2)}$.

Other checked ancient metrics are not integer. However we get a strange result for geodetic metrics. The large circle diameter is 16.182 arc seconds or 10.Phi arc seconds...an interesting coincidence. The circle circumference is 50.83 or 10.Pi.Phi arc seconds. We have 10, the Holy Tetrachys of the Pythagorean Brotherhood, Pi and Phi together, a powerful symbolic number in geodetic units (see **Footnote A** and Appendix 3).The circumference of the small circle is 32.03 arc seconds. Some coincidences simply beggar belief, so we pass on.

The stones at Corporation Road have similar Venus connections (not including the modern association with local ladies of the night). We have five remaining stones in an area already under urban development in 1872. Perhaps there were more stones once. Upper Beckwith St. has open fields at the time. Stones s1, s2, s3, s4 like the Beckwith stones form a main axis. All possible lines have similar azimuths.
s1s2 s4 has an azimuth of 116 d and declination of -15.1 d
s1s3 azimuth 118 d declination -16.25 d
s3s4 azimuth 115 dec -14.6 d

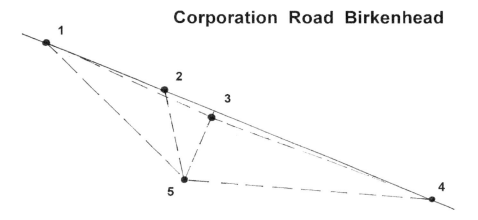

Corporation Road Birkenhead

These declinations are familiar from Beckwith St. and elsewhere. s1s3 declination we interpreted as -32.5 / 2 = -16.25 d, the mid-declination of Venus rise between the equinox line and extreme southern rising at -32.5 d. Just to confirm this note that s5s3 has a declination of 33 d, extreme northern declination of Venus rise.

Footnote A : The Pythagoreans venerated 10 because 10 = 1+2+3+4, the sum of the first 4 integers but 10 (fingers) is also the common base for counting (along with 5 and 20 in some early cultures). However '10' hides a deeper property if we apply Pythagoras' *own* theorem.

$Phi^2 + e^2 = 10.0066$. Our modest circle hosts the Tetrachys and the three great irrational constants of nature: Pi, e & Phi. That is odd indeed.

s3s4 and s1s2s4 have declinations -14.6 d and -15.1 d and a mean of -14.85 d. However the mid-declination moonrise between equinox and southern major standstill is - 29.13 / 2 = - 14.6 d. We have another probable lunar declination in s5s4 at azimuth 98d dec - 4.8 d. From Beckwith St. we know that – 5.1 d declination marks the extreme southern equinox moonrise. We also have s1s5 at declination – 28 d but this is close to extreme southern moonrise at major standstill declination -29.1 d.

s2s3 has an azimuth of 124 d at declination -19.4 d which we see matches moonrise at southern minor standstill, declination -19.13 d. Finally we have s2s5 at azimuth 351d declination 36.1 d which we also saw at Beckwith St. We interpreted this as the setting point of a near-circumpolar clock star.

We have 5 stones which give 5 x (5-1) /2 = 10 possible 2 stones lines. Three lines through s1, s2, s4 have identical declinations of - 15.1 d. Nine of the 10 lines match obvious lunar or Venus events but 4 lines are at declination 33 / 2, not in our original target list. One line may be a stellar marker. So we take 5 hits out of 10 lines. This result is again well beyond chance.

$$(1/12)^5 \text{ x } (11/12)^5 \text{ x } 10! / (5! \text{ } 5!) = 6.6 \text{ x } 10^{-4}, \text{ odds of 1 to 1515.}$$

Considering the formal 19th century 'grid' design of Birkenhead we note that main east – west roads such as Clevelend Street and Corporation Road are at azimuth 115 d and declination -14.6 = -29.2 / 2 d (midway moonrise) and the main cross roads such as Victoria Street and Duke Street are at azimuth 24 – 25 d and declination ~32.8 d (Venus extreme north rising). We noted that the extreme northern rising of Venus is at an accurate right angle to the mid way declination of moonrise between equinox rising and southern major standstill rising. This relationship is clearly recorded in the local stones.

If the key 'new' roads respected the old stone rows in the fields at Upper Beckwith St. and Corporation Road this means the formal rectangular grid layout of Birkenhead is based on the movements of Venus and the moon !

Did the planners know? Images of 19th century, city scale, 'Druid' follies designed by an obsessive (but influential) Masonic cabal again surfaced unbidden, in the author's mind. The author finds this Da Vinci Code, 'Dan Brown' interpretation disturbing.

It is hopefully more likely that the new roads followed ancient field or property boundaries which had long been marked by these ancient (and respected) stones.

A careful analysis of the layout of these sites is required before more can be said but early Birkenhead is worth exploring further. Much more may remain. Perhaps the Norse settler, Ufaldi, was merely taking over a much earlier and well remembered site when he developed 'Ufaldi's Green' in what is now Birkenhead Park. The Park has been put forward for World Heritage status as the 'first' civic public park. If the site is also Neolithic or Bronze Age it would seem that status is doubly deserved.

Printed in Great Britain
by Amazon